Daniel Pinfor

Jasper 🐾

Let Me Tell You about Jasper…

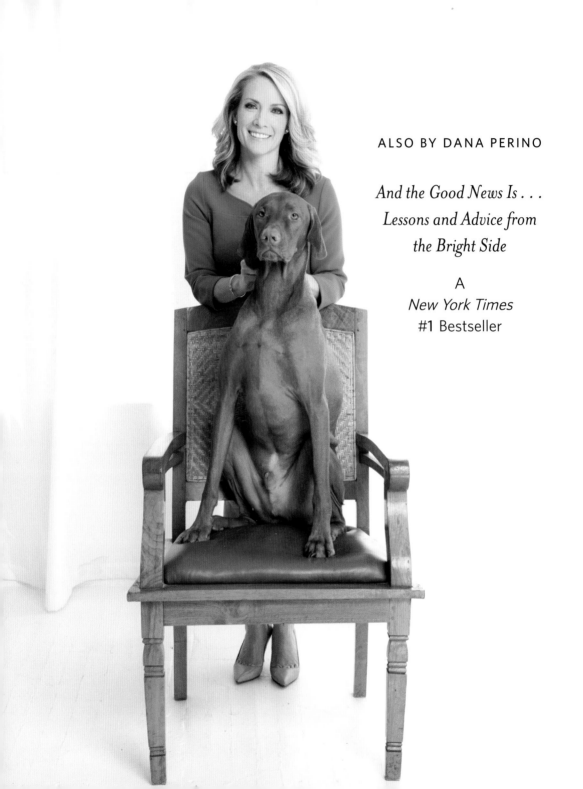

ALSO BY DANA PERINO

*And the Good News Is . . .
Lessons and Advice from
the Bright Side*

A
New York Times
#1 Bestseller

Let Me Tell You about Jasper...

How My Best Friend Became America's Dog

DANA PERINO

TWELVE

New York • Boston

Twelve
Hachette Book Group
1290 Avenue of the Americas, New York, NY 10104
twelvebooks.com
twitter.com/twelvebooks

First Edition: October 2016

Twelve is an imprint of Grand Central Publishing. The Twelve name and logo are trademarks of Hachette Book Group, Inc.

The publisher is not responsible for websites (or their content) that are not owned by the publisher.

Library of Congress Cataloging-in-Publication Data has been applied for.

ISBNs: 978-1-4555-6710-2 (hardcover), 978-1-4555-6712-6 (ebook),
978-1-4789-7089-7 (signed edition)

Printed in the United States of America

Q-MA

10 9 8 7 6 5 4 3 2 1

To my grandfather, Leo E. Perino,

who taught me about dignity, patriotism, and
love for animals

Red Eye, Summer of 2013

GREG: Actress Eva Mendes tells *New York* magazine that she wishes the tabloids would blur the faces of her dog Hugo, like British rags do with celebrities' kids.

She says, "I'll go somewhere and they'll be like, 'Hey, Hugo.' And I'm like, 'How do you know Hugo's name?' That's so creepy."

To throw off the paparazzi, she now has someone else walk Hugo.

Dana, I go to you first for no particular reason whatsoever. Why must your friends, family, and Twitter followers be kept abreast of everything your precious Jasper does?

DANA: I know that I'm a dog bore, but I embrace it. It gives me great joy. I love all the pictures. And you know what? I'll make Jasper "America's Dog." He is for everybody, and I'll share him with the world.

Look at that face! And he's got that little ear and he's so cute!

People *adore* Jasper and they say, don't stop tweeting pictures of Jasper just because Greg Gutfeld makes fun of you.

GREG: Would you want your dog's face blurred?

DANA: No. Actually, you know what? People recognize Jasper more than they recognize me at the park, and I love that.

They're like, "OMG is that Jasper!? We *love* Jasper."

So I think I have finally achieved something in life. Finally!

Contents

Introduction · XI

LET ME TELL YOU ABOUT JASPER · 1

My Dog, the Celebrity · 3

Dog Owners "Get" Each Other · 12

Who Needs Twitter? I Did, Apparently. · 14

What Kind of Dog Is Jasper? A Hungarian Vizsla · 18

Are You Jasper's Mom? · 20

Henry Vizsla · 21

Bringing Henry Home · 25

Peter Gets Arrested—Because of the Dog · 38

One Last Swim · 44

Nicknames · 54

Jasper · 56

Dog on the Loose—and Dragging a Table · 66

Separation Anxiety—But Whose? · 68

Dog Park Rules · 76

The Protest Pee · 84

You're Back! Here's a Stuffed Animal Carcass · 87

Dana's Personal Tips for Dog Training · 92

Dogus Interruptus   96

Nonstop Jasper Chatter   102

"The Vizsla"   104

Jasper and Water   106

Not Just a City Dog   111

A Day in the Life of Jasper   118

Jasper Grows Up   124

INTRODUCING @FIVEFAN PHOTOSHOPS   127

Portraits of a Dog   133

Play Like a Champion, Train Like an Underdog   140

Out and About   162

Jingle Bells and Jack-o-Lanterns   170

The Secret Life of Jasper   180

Collect Them All!   196

Political Hot Dog   204

American Classics   216

Jasper's Glamorous TV Life   244

Acknowledgments   257

Introduction

When I wrote *And the Good News Is...*, I had an entire chapter about dogs—the ones I grew up with in Wyoming and Colorado, the one I had to give away at college, and the ones I've raised with my husband. I loved that chapter. I was proud of it, too. It had great detail, funny stories, and descriptions of the life lessons I'd learned from being around dogs (more, I think, than I've learned from humans). I thought it fit perfectly into my book that blended my memoir with my best career advice.

The problem was, my editor, Sean Desmond, needed me to cut about ten thousand words from the draft manuscript. I spent a weekend trying to trim off that length, but the text was pretty tight. I got frustrated. I couldn't find a way to delete that much copy.

Finally, I stepped back and took a long look at the dog chapter. It was several thousand words long. I eyed it for the chopping block, but I couldn't bring down the hatchet. I slept on it (the book, not the hatchet). The deadline loomed.

I used my foolproof method of decision-making, praying for a clear idea of how to solve my problem. When I woke up, I knew what I needed to do.

I printed the dog chapter and took it with me to Sean's office near Grand Central Station in Manhattan.

"This may be the hardest thing I do, and it is breaking my heart," I said. "But here you go. You can have the dog chapter. Without it, we can make the word count."

I tossed the chapter onto his desk.

While Sean isn't a dog person, he knew it was quite a sacrifice.

"I think this is the right decision," he said. "And I promise you, one day there will be a dog book."

And true to his word, here we are.

So let me tell you about Jasper—how my best friend became "America's Dog."

Let Me Tell You about Jasper...

DOG OF THE YEAR

TIME

JASPER
AMERICA'S DOG

My Dog, the Celebrity

Jasper is a four-year-old Hungarian Vizsla. My husband, Peter, and I brought him home to New York City from Maryland in June 2012 when he was nine weeks old. No one has ever made me laugh more—he's a beautiful little rascal. (My dog, I mean, not Peter. Though, now that I think about it…)

He's also a bit of a celebrity. I didn't set out to make Jasper a star; it just happened, and almost overnight. He's got that "certain something," and together, over time, Jasper and I have connected with more people and their pets than I ever thought possible. I wanted to write this book because I'm touched by the human connection that we can make with each other through our dogs.

It is a bit wonderful that through television and social media, Jasper and I became friends with so many people across the country. I enjoy interacting with my followers and fans, and I really feel that we have modern-day friendships—people I've never met, but that I've come to know over time through short digital interactions. It has widened my circle of people I talk to, and it's deepened my appreciation for people from all walks of life. I now get a chance to communicate with people I wouldn't have ever known; the Internet has given us a way to connect and network that didn't exist before. We're all neighbors now (with the proper amount of fencing to keep things friendly).

Often this new group of people has cheered me up or warmed my heart just when I needed it. Working in politics and live cable television can be stressful, and switching off at the end of the day isn't always easy.

Jasper's following has actually given me a way to set aside the work portion of my day and exchange some messages with my electronic friends, which helps me keep grounded and cheerful.

I've long used dogs as a buffer between my work and personal life, though I didn't realize it until I sat down and really thought about how much I appreciate dogs. On my way to work, I see dogs out for their afternoon walks and it always makes me smile. Dogs have a way of softening my hard edges.

And I've found that no matter what the controversies or issues of the day that we discuss—and argue about—on television and online, dogs are the great equalizer. Just when it feels like we are so polarized as a country between right and left, and that we can't get along, remember that we have a few things in common—and for millions of us, that is our love for our pets (this includes cats—I guess*). Sometimes, if you can't get along with anyone or you have strife in a relationship, find common ground through your dogs: hit the dog park and reconnect. It's certainly better than a four-hour heart-to-heart in Starbucks, ending in an awkward hug and a secret promise to yourself that you will block this person from your phone.

Throughout my life, dogs have helped me to connect with people. I think back to my time at the cattle and Quarter Horse ranch my family runs in the Black Hills near Newcastle, Wyoming, and how we didn't do anything without a pack of dogs around. They helped with ranch work, herding the cattle or warning us if there was danger. And they were our companions—they followed us everywhere, and we loved having them around.

My grandfather was born on the ranch and dogs were an important part of the operation. He was an excellent dog trainer. He could teach a young pup to respond to several different whistles and get them to perform their tasks depending on what job he needed them to do. In the evenings

---

*Kidding!

No matter where I was, at my home in Colorado or at my grandparents' ranch in Wyoming, our dogs were always with us. That's my mom and me with Joco in Colorado, and my cousin with one of the ranch puppies named Coop....I miss those pants!

as the sun went down, he would go to the yard outside the gate and the dogs would follow. If he needed them to bring in the mares, he'd whistle and point and off they'd go, tearing over the hill to do their job. Soon enough, the horses would come up over the ridge and the dogs would get them into the smaller fenced corral by the barn. My grandpa would chastise them if they nipped at the mares' heels too much, and then he'd reward them with praise and a scrub of the scruff of their necks when they finished their jobs. The dogs lived to please him—they were very devoted to their boss. Loyalty goes both ways.

My grandfather, Leo E. Perino, my Uncle Matt (who runs the ranch today) and my late Uncle Tom (who died from cancer in 2006) with their working dogs. FROM LEFT TO RIGHT: *Skip, Robin, Blue, Rocky. And then there's Moe, my grandma's house dog. Moe wanted to be a big dog, and he knew how to photobomb!*

My grandfather's final two dogs, Ray and Floyd, were game to go at all times—they loved to hop in the back of the pickup, or they'd run alongside us if we went for a horseback ride. We didn't worry when they took off for a little side trip. Sometimes they came back filthy with the red dirt of the Black Hills caked into their fur; other times they came bustling back as if a coyote or a bear had told them to get the heck out of Dodge. At night, they bedded down on the porch and kept watch on the house. And they were ready to go before the sun came up.

My grandma had her own dog. His name was Moe, and he was a spunky miniature poodle who enjoyed house privileges. But though he slept in the warm house, during the day he tried to run with the big dogs on the ranch when they were out working with my grandpa and my uncles. Moe used to get groomed, and I remember my grandfather saying that Moe was so embarrassed by the sissy poodle cut and ribbons in his ears that as soon as he jumped out of the car, he'd find the freshest pile of manure to roll in and cover the scent of his trip to town. We all laughed…well, everyone but my grandma.

We adored our dogs. We gushed over new puppies and cherished the older dogs. Our shared love for dogs helped keep the family close.

At my childhood homes in Denver and Parker, Colorado, we had Joco, an apricot poodle. He was named for one of the homesteaders that came over from Italy around when

Me with my mom, my grandparents from the ranch, and my great-grandmother. We were in Denver—the only time Great Grandma made the trip to the big city. Joco had to be in the shot, too.

my great-grandparents did in the late 1800s. Unfortunately, the original Joco didn't stay in America. He went back to his homeland after the harsh winters and loneliness of ranching got to him. But by all accounts he was quite a character, and he became a legend in the Black Hills.

My sister, Angie, and I taught Joco (the dog) how to dance, dressed him in baby clothes, walked him around the neighborhood, and begged our parents to take him with us in the car whenever we could. Joco watched us play in the backyard and crawled up into my sister's crib when she took a nap. He sat in the bathroom when my sister had the croup and my mom ran the hot water into the tub, hoping the steam would break up her cough. I think Joco believed he was our little brother.

LEFT: *Me as a baby with my dad and Joco.* RIGHT: *My mom said she will never forget this moment when she brought my baby sister, Angie, home. All of her babies were together for the first time.*

Angie, my mom, Joco, and me. Nice coveralls, Angie!

When we were a bit older, we were responsible for taking care of him when we got home from school. In turn, he kept us safe, especially during the dark winter evenings before our parents got home.

Dogs get sweeter as they age—they sleep more, and they need more care as they get sick or their joints get stiff. Joco developed seizures when he was older, and it was terrible to watch. There was really nothing we could do but try to calm him until it passed. My sister and I would keep an anxious eye on him when we were home alone—we were so worried Joco would have a seizure when our parents weren't there. So we often wrapped him in a blanket and sat on the floor with him while we watched TV until they got home. Joco slept in our mom and dad's room on a little pillow with this avocado-green pillowcase—it's funny what we remember from our childhoods. I can picture him curled up on that pillow like it was yesterday.

Joco had a good life, and he lived to be seventeen, which is a pretty good age for any dog. I was a junior in high school when he died. We'd discussed that he was going to need to be euthanized because he was so sick. But still it is a shock when you have to do it.

My mom had to take Joco by herself that day, which is something she said she still regrets. It was harder than she imagined. After school I met up with her in the Safeway parking lot and she was crushed, her eyes really red from crying. Back then, the vet had you drop off your dog and he or she took it from there. My mom said she had the hardest time leaving him there and that she still thinks about it. Today, it is more common to be there with your family pet when you have to put them down.

For my mom, that day was a real marker. All of her kids—me, my sister, and Joco—had been together for seventeen years, and his death was a blow. It hit us all pretty hard.

And while we'd known animals on the ranch that had died over the years, Joco's death was my first real understanding of grief from loss. Looking back, Joco was also my first real understanding of unconditional love and caring for another living being. He was a good boy, and I still miss him.

At that time, I was getting ready to go to college, so I wasn't thinking about getting another dog. But my sister was despondent and lonely without Joco. She's usually so chipper that it was hard to watch her be so sad.

Angie and Yukon (the sock stealer!). Yukon kept my sister company when I left for college.

One day, my mom and dad took her to the Dumb Friends League (an animal shelter, not where Denverites send Cowboys fans) "just to look" and, of course, they brought home an "Eskimo dog." My sister named her Yukon, and she was bright white with dark blue eyes. One thing I remember about Yukie is that she loved socks. Hardly any of our socks kept their match after she came to live with us.

Yukon brightened up the house and even got along with our two calico cats. (One rescue we conned our parents into letting sleep in the house "just one night—come ON, it's Christmas Eve!" And another I secretly brought back from the ranch in a cardboard box and hid in my room for three days before my mom and dad found out. Hoo-boy, they were not happy with me—but they let me keep her.)

In college, a boyfriend bought me a puppy—it was a gift of love, but it was totally wrong. I tried to take care of it in my dorm room (which didn't allow dogs) and over time it was clear that the puppy, Sugar, would need to go to another home. I was heartbroken to give her away and ashamed that I'd put a dog in that position. Ever since, I've counseled young people to wait until they're more established and ready to have a pet. (That means you, sweet millennials.)

Dogs are a constant responsibility and they deserve proper care and attention—they need exercise and companionship. And their vet bills can get expensive. It's better to wait. And if you're ever in a situation where the dog becomes a burden or a chore, it's time to realize you may not be ready for a dog. That's what happened to me with Sugar, and I've never forgotten how rotten I felt then. But I'm glad I learned that lesson.

Throughout my childhood and then after I was married, I've always had dogs. Most of my friends I've met either because of our dogs or because we bonded over mine. Dogs help me have more fun in life, to live more in the here and now, which sometimes is difficult for a worrier and a planner like me.

I laugh more when I'm around dogs. I take in my surroundings and appreciate the beauty around me. I can just . . . be. I find serenity, where I'm not worried about yesterday or tomorrow but enjoy the feeling of really living. Without dogs, I don't know if I'd experience that joy very often. I'd probably need to go live in Tibet or something.

It is also freeing to go for a walk with my dog and not worry about how my hair looks. I often go without any makeup (but I do wear sunscreen!). Like other dog owners, I have a whole set of "dog park clothes," and let's just say most people wouldn't wear them anywhere else. I've not been clean a full day since I've had dogs—and it doesn't bother me a bit. Again, out at the dog park, the humans are on equal albeit shabby footing. There's no pretension or competition. There's just fun.

And having dogs has made me lighten up around the house—it's impossible to keep the floors spotless at all times. Dogs track in mud and dead leaves (and, sometimes, stuff that looks like mud but smells). I've learned to let go a bit and not try to pick up after every time we go out for a walk. So you can't eat off my floor—that's okay, we have plates!

One of the things I love about Jasper is that he doesn't know he's popular. In my line of work, I'm around a lot of famous people, yet Jasper is probably more recognized than most of them. And he's got no idea. To him, he's just our dog (though some have asked if he thinks he's a "real boy," given his facial expressions and the way he behaves and poses...and he acts a lot more human than some of the people I've met in politics along the way).

And to think I almost didn't even know how to share him with anyone.

Dog Owners "Get" Each Other

DOG OWNERS HAVE A LOT IN COMMON. They're silly about their dogs—and their dogs let them *be* silly, which is part of the joy.

Peter and I are our goofiest when we're with or talking about Jasper. We make silly voices and we sing to him all the time.

A staple song is one we brought from England and used to sing to Henry. It's the signal that we're about to head out for a walk:

Do you want to go to the park? Woof woof.
Do you want to run, jump, and bark? Woof woof.
Do you want to go; do you want to go…(pause for effect)
Do you want to go to the park? Woof woof!

As a puppy, Jasper loved to be carried and he would rest his head on Peter's shoulder. I wish I could still carry him like this today!

Henry would bark once for please if we sang that. Jasper just goes to the door and waits to get his "necklace" on (also known as a collar).

We've even made up lyrics to some of the classics—such as "Take it Easy" by The Eagles . . . with a twist:

Well, you've been…running 'round the park
Tryin' to loosen your bark
You've got squirrels and pigeons on your mind…

***

*Some you want to race and
Some you want to chase,
But they all get up a tree in time.*

***

*Jasper Baby…Jasper Baby…
Don't let the sound of your own
bark make you crazy . . .*

***

*You can run and you can play
You can sit, lie down, and stay,
Or just sleep on the couch all day
Jasper Baby*

***

*You love to take a nap
With your head on someone's lap
It's the place you love to be*

***

*Squeezin' up so close
With your cold, wet nose
I love to have you cuddle me . . .
Jasper Baby . . . Jasper Baby . . .
I gotta know that your sweet love is gonna save me.*

*Jasper in Central Park
looking for fish.*

It goes on and on . . . and once you sing that song, it could be in your head forever. Consider that fair warning. I tried to sing it on *The Five* for my "One More Thing" but I choked and collapsed in laughter. Only Jasper thinks I have a good voice.

Who Needs Twitter?
I Did, Apparently.

When I first left the White House in 2009, I didn't have a Twitter account. I didn't even want one. I couldn't imagine that it was something that would help me in my work.

But a young staff member of mine convinced me it would be good for business. I said okay, you can set it up, but don't expect me to tweet nonsense.

"How about I teach you how to post pictures of your dog?" she asked.

That got my attention. (This girl will go far.)

"Show me," I said.

After that, I was hooked. I had a lot of fun taking pictures and coming up with clever captions. I started getting more followers and friends and making connections with people who might have been on the other side of the political spectrum from me—but who cared? We loved our dogs. We bonded over them.

🐾

Jasper was a somewhat famous puppy before he even came to live with us. I built up the anticipation with tweets about his progress and how Peter and I were buying all the gear you need to help a puppy grow into an adult dog.

Jasper made his debut on *The Five* as a sleepy puppy at just two months old, and a star was born. I brought him on set and when we were back from commercial break, I showed him off for the camera. He looked right into

the lens with his deep blue eyes (a Vizsla is born with blue eyes that eventually turn amber). He snuggled into me. Hearts melted.

Jasper has tons of personality and is as photogenic as any dog I've known. On Jasper's birthdays, my producer lets him come on the show and he sits on a chair, for the most part,

Baby Jasper with his baby blue eyes. And his elephant. I always wonder what dogs are thinking . . .

wearing a bow tie collar, and you would think he knows exactly what he's doing when he looks into the teleprompter. He's certainly better behaved than Gutfeld.

During the first year of Jasper's life, I started noticing a change in my interaction with people. I'd come to Fox News after serving in the White House for President George W. Bush, and many people knew me as the first Republican woman to serve as the White House press secretary. If I was recognized, folks would ask me to give my regards to President and Mrs. Bush (and those few that wanted me to send a different message got "the look").

Then in 2012, it changed to questions like "How's Jasper?" on the street or "Did you bring Jasper?" from TSA agents. Even in New York City, it went from "Hey, lady, get out of the way!" to "Hey, lady, nice dog. Now get out of the way!"

My most prized possession: President Bush's portrait of Jasper as a puppy. It's the one item that is to be saved in case of an emergency.
PHOTO ON RIGHT, CREDIT:
BARRY MORGENSTEIN

At speeches, the first question I got was usually about Jasper, and I started to realize that it was my pet that was helping me connect with people in ways that weren't partisan or political.

And I really liked it; a welcome change from talking about politics all the time. Jasper was a professional icebreaker. And he has saved me from hours of small talk about the weather…or politics!

On social media, I'd get messages encouraging me to keep posting pictures of Jasper, even though sometimes my colleagues teased me about my obsession. (You should hear about *their* obsessions. For instance…er, never mind.)

After he was nicknamed America's Dog on *Red Eye*, some fans would thank me for being willing to share him with them, especially if they couldn't have a dog of their own. They'd tell me they looked forward to Jasper's morning posts and shared the experience with their kids or grandchildren.

When on a whim I made a calendar of Jasper pictures and printed copies for my co-hosts for Christmas presents, I was surprised how many people sent messages asking for one. I'd just done it on a bit of a lark—but the love for Jasper had really turned into something.

Jasper and I posed for the cover of Life and Dog *magazine in 2014. I love this photo because it looks like I think that he and I are married!*

What Kind of Dog Is Jasper?
A Hungarian Vizsla

UP UNTIL THE LAST SEVERAL YEARS, VIZSLAS WERE NOT WELL KNOWN IN THE UNITED STATES. I used to be asked, "What kind of dog is that?" but now, with more awareness of the breed, I'm often asked, "Is that a Vizsla?" It is!

Vizslas are sporting dogs. They are sleek, muscular, and have only one coat of fur, which is silky to the touch. Their eyes are blue as puppies but blend in with their coat as they reach adulthood, and they have a liver-colored nose.

Vizslas are very loyal and were bred to stay close to their owners. They do not like to be left by themselves or to sleep alone. "If you own a Vizsla, it lives on top of your head," they say in Hungary. Don't we know it. Jasper rarely lets us out of his sight (so there's very little privacy in our house, if you know what I mean), and whenever I sit,

he's there in an instant, right next to or on top of me.

The Vizsla is a Hungarian dog with a long history, going all the way back to the Magyar tribes that came across Asia in the tenth century. It's reported that the breed dwindled in size during wars in the region. At one point in the late nineteenth century, only about a dozen Vizslas were alive in Hungary. Thankfully, enough dogs were saved and the Vizsla was rehabilitated by some determined breeders.

Over the years, local nobility controlled the breed and rarely let a Vizsla leave Hungary, even though other Europeans very much wanted to import the dogs. In fact, it wasn't until the Russian invasion of Hungary that the Hungarians started to send Vizslas to other countries, with the hope of preserving the breed. Since the dogs were tied to the aristocracy, they worried about their survival.

JASPER
AMERICA'S DOG

Soon after World War II, Vizslas started coming to the United States. Interest in the breed grew, and just seventy years later, one special Vizsla was nicknamed America's Dog!

A fan of *The Five* told me her grandchildren call Vizslas "Jasper dogs," and Jasper and Henry even get mentions on the Wikipedia page about the breed. I love all dogs, but I'm glad I've had the chance to get to know the Vizsla.

It's too bad: they always seem to get robbed of first prize at the dog shows. But no matter—they're number one in my book. 🐾

Are You Jasper's Mom?

I knew that Jasper had really become more popular than me when in the fall of 2015, a jogger in Central Park stopped us and said, "That's a beautiful dog," and we thanked him. Recognizing my voice, he said, "Wait—is that *the* Jasper?"

I said yes, and he asked if he could get a picture. Peter took the man's phone and I moved to get in the picture when I realized that he didn't want me in it. He just wanted a photo with Jasper. (I wasn't offended! Although I hope that photo isn't up on some strange website hosted overseas.)

Yet it was at a holiday party thrown by Megyn Kelly for her show's staff and contributors that I fully realized that I was no longer recognized as a presidential press secretary; I was now known first and foremost as Jasper's mom.

Megyn had created a trivia game and she divided the room in two. She read aloud questions about her production team and her regular guests. The prize? Cash! And bragging rights.

I had fun listening from the back, shouting a few answers. And then I was really touched by this one:

"Before there was Jasper, there was…"

My throat caught. I thought that no one would know the answer.

But Vincenza Carovillano, a makeup artist and a friend for years, did.

"HENRY!" she yelled.

She was right.

Before there was Jasper, there was Henry.

Henry Vizsla

I met my husband on an airplane in August 1997. We were assigned seats next to each other and were the last two to board a flight I almost missed and that he nearly didn't take.

Peter was forty-three, a successful British businessman, twice divorced, and the father of two grown children. I was twenty-five—just getting my career underway as a press secretary on Capitol Hill in Washington, D.C.—and going through what I call a quarter-life crisis, a period of anxiety and confusion that most young women have after college (ladies—the crisis ends, believe me).

While I was open to meeting someone, I was fairly career focused, and Peter thought he would never marry again. Besides, we lived on different continents. Neither of us planned on falling in love on that flight from Denver to Chicago, but that's what happened. I call it "love at first flight."

Our romance was quick and intense. We were lovesick. For ten days after we met, I couldn't eat or sleep or concentrate at work. I couldn't even read the novels I checked out from the Library of Congress.

Peter had fallen hard for yours truly, and was waiting for me to respond to an e-mail he'd sent, but his office's new server had kicked it back without him knowing. Over a week later, he was on vacation when he found out about the server. Worried, he drove out of his way and miles longer than he intended that day just to resend the e-mail to me. He had a feeling I was going to get over him before he even had a chance to woo me.

Peter was right. Back in D.C., I was worried that my love connection on that plane was just a fantasy. After not hearing from him for nearly two weeks, I decided that I had to push him completely out of my mind. It was a hot August day and I went down to the courtyard in the Rayburn House Office Building and sat outside and read *The Agony and the Ecstasy* by Irving Stone (the title was appropriate for my mood).

At 1 p.m., I closed the book and went upstairs, feeling free and refocused on my job. I booted up my computer and, you guessed it, there was Peter's e-mail. It hadn't been too late.

The rest was quick history. From October to May, we wrote romantic letters—yes, real handwritten letters with stamps and everything. They go through this service called "the mail" and it's the most amazing thing! And we spoke every day, too (the phone bills were high but Peter never complained or commented on the cost).

Peter came to the United States nine times, and I went over to visit him twice, the second time to pick out a flat where we'd live (yes, I was already calling it a flat). I came back and got up the courage to resign from my Capitol Hill job and tell my parents I was moving to the UK. To my pleasant surprise, everyone was supportive (once they revived my father). I was energized and relaxed, confident and contented. This was love. This was being a grown-up.

While he worked during the day, I read books and surfed the Internet. (I didn't realize that at that time in England you paid by the minute for dial-up service. Peter gently asked me to be more conservative with my browsing.)

I took to cooking vegetarian meals out of the *Moosewood* cookbook (because meat was expensive and I really didn't know how to cook it), and I still have the chart Peter made for me for easy reference between Celsius and Fahrenheit when I needed to use the oven.

I learned how to make Greek pilaf, polenta pizza pie, and black bean soup. To this day if you ask Peter what his favorite meal is that I make, he says quesadillas. Imagine! He'd never had one, so he thought I was the Julia Child of Mexican cheese sandwiches.

On weekends, he took me to all the places I'd read about—Windermere in the Lake District, Durham Cathedral, Tintagel Castle where King Arthur is said to have met with the Knights of the Round Table, and the Roman city of Chester with its beautiful Tudor buildings. (I think he figured it was cheaper to take me with him than to leave me home with the expensive Internet service.) On occasion, I traveled with him to visit clients all over Europe, and it was on one of those trips that we found our next mutual love: the Vizsla.

Both of us had been wanting a dog but were trying to keep an open mind on the breed. Peter was partial to a black lab and I was into Weimaraners (I love William Wegman's photographs).

On a visit to Switzerland, Peter had a meeting with a client named Heiner (German for Henry). He invited us to his chalet and said I could play with the dogs while they met. (I felt a little indignant—I mean, I used to advise members of Congress and now I was reduced to babysitting the dogs! However, the dogs *were* better listeners.)

We pulled up and there were two russet hounds that had the shape of a pointer, like a red Weimaraner. One of Heiner's dogs was seven years old, the other just a three-month-old pup.

"What kind of dogs are these?" was our first question.

"These are Hungarian Vizslas. To me, they are the best dogs in the world," he said.

I don't remember much of the business meeting. I spent time playing with that puppy and kissing its head. Heiner told us all about the breed. We asked if he knew any breeders. He did; in fact, one of the breeders lived in Scotland and had a new litter (that is, the breeder's *dog* had a new litter).

We hadn't even left Heiner's driveway when Peter phoned the Scottish breeder, Helen MacCauley. She had one male pup left.

"We'll take him," he said, cutting her off when she tried to explain the attributes of the puppies and how they'd make for excellent show dogs. The sire had won Best in Breed at Crufts the year before, and she thought we might want to show our dog.

"We just plan to love him," Peter said, giving me a thumbs-up and one of his biggest smiles. We were getting a puppy.

Bringing Henry Home

On a rainy Friday in July, Peter and I drove to Scotland on our way to pick up our new family member.

We stayed overnight in a small village at a country bed-and-breakfast. It was about fifty degrees outside and felt colder in the house. The constant drizzle had drilled holes into my bones.

The owner showed us around and noted the gas heater in the fireplace.

"But you won't be needing that!" she said. Utility bills in the United Kingdom are really high, so "put another sweater on" is the best way to stay warm and save some pennies.

As soon as she left, I told Peter to crank it up. The Scots have no idea how acclimated they are to cold weather.

The next morning, we headed to the Vizsla breeder's home. I had butterflies.

We'd already picked out a name—Henry—in memory of one of my favorite novels, *The Autobiography of King Henry VIII* by Margaret George, and the man that first introduced us to the Vizsla. It felt properly British and perfect.

All the dogs were pledged to new owners, but we were the first to arrive, so we had our choice of four males. The MacCauleys led us to the kitchen and placed those four in a pen and we got in it. Two of them we eliminated right away—I don't remember why, because they were all gorgeous. I was looking for a calm, sweet puppy. One was adorable and jumping up and down around Peter; the other sat by my feet and looked up with blue eyes. I had a gut instinct to choose the calm one, but we couldn't decide.

"Let's have lunch and you can try again after that," Helen said.

We ate sandwiches and soup, my favorite English meal (seriously—I love it). When we went back into the kitchen, she presented the final two pups and we stood there—the same thing happened. The calm one came to me, sat at my feet, and looked up, never breaking eye contact. The rambunctious one went to Peter and tried to scramble up his leg.

I trusted my instinct and said that we should go with the bigger, calmer one. Peter agreed.

It turns out we made the right decision. Henry was born smart, sweet, and dignified—a rarity in any species.

As we made to leave, I got teary on behalf of Henry's mom because he was going to be the first of her eleven puppies to leave the litter. Helen had tears in her eyes, too, as the mama dog (called a dam) was her pet and we thought the dam was sad to see little Henry leave.

Henry came home the same way Jasper would fourteen years later—sacked out on my lap. Peter preferred to drive since I was a bit shaky on the other side of the road in Britain. That worked out well for me—more puppy time!

"You're his mom now," she said.

When we got in the black Isuzu Trooper to drive home, Helen told me to take out my earrings in case he nibbled at them. And before we left she said, "Remember, the love you give them you get twice as much in return." Peter insists this is an understatement.

Henry was good in the car—he just let me hold him and he tucked his nose into my neck and slept like that for hours.

Peter drove most of the way but insisted I take a turn at the wheel so that he could hold and bond with his new puppy. I was an okay driver in the UK, but with me on the wrong side of the car and the wrong side of the road, Peter took over again after just forty-five minutes (he'd seemed calm enough, but I noticed he was clutching rosary beads and muttering to himself).

I called later to let the MacCauleys know we'd arrived back in England safely and to inquire about how Henry's dam reacted to him being taken away from the litter.

"She didn't even notice," she said, and we laughed, though I felt slightly offended on Henry's behalf.

I really was Henry's mom.

I bonded with Henry immediately. I was home all day with him while Peter worked. Taking care of a puppy is time-consuming. I watched him constantly, potty trained him (no comment on which newspaper we used), and gave him the best food prescribed at the time (plus a raw egg for a

shiny coat). There were days when Peter came home and I still hadn't done the dishes from the morning. "What has she been *doing* all day?" he thought, but dared not ask until years later.

I carried Henry around when he was perfectly capable of walking on his own, and I tried to coax him into the garden on rainy days though he didn't want to get wet. I sat at the computer and refreshed the Drudge Report over and over. (It was 1998, folks! The Lewinsky scandal was a huge story.)

In our English flat, I tried to make it feel a bit like home with lots of pictures and a painting of the American flag that I purchased at Eastern Market in Washington, D.C. when I worked on Capitol Hill.

Meanwhile, Henry slept in my lap and rested his chin on my wrist. (Henry was skeptical—he may have been a dog but even he knew what the definition of "is" is.)

If it was too rainy outside I would play tug-of-war with his puppy toys, throw the ball down the hallway over and over, and then we'd play our favorite game—I'd sit in front of the couch and Henry would come over and put his rear end by my feet. Then I'd launch him across the room and he'd twirl around in the air, landing on all four paws. He never tired of the game, and my legs got a good workout.

I wanted my dog to be well trained, so when he was very young, I taught him to bark once for please and twice for thank you, to give a high five instead of shaking, to sit, stay, and play dead (all of this worked on Peter, too, by the way).

Henry was taught to wait to eat his food until I gave him permission. And when he was hand-fed treats, I'd say, "Gentle, gentle," and he had such a soft mouth that when my friends' toddlers fed him Cheerios one by one we didn't worry that he'd snap at them and nip their fingers. When Peter came home, I would show off all of Henry's new tricks. (And I'd talk nonstop for a couple of hours since I didn't have anyone else to talk to all day. I know . . . poor Peter.)

I fell hopelessly in love with Henry, and it deepened my love for Peter, too. I watched him be so patient with Henry, taking him outside at any time of day or night without complaint. I loved how he could put Henry on his forearm, the puppy's chin in his palm, the four legs dangling over the sides, and walk him all around the flat.

Which shows how Henry allowed us to be a little silly, too. We needed help on that front since we were adults and had kind of forgotten how to play like kids.

Plus, having Henry got us outside together, no matter the weather. We spent hours on the beach at Lytham-St. Anne's when the tide was out, letting Henry race between us to get all of his energy out before we went to bed.

Henry and I were blown about on a trip to the Lake District when he was just three months old. For fourteen years, Henry, Peter and I were inseparable.

Peter and Henry in Cornwall —one of my favorite pictures of them. Peter had wanted a dog for many years, and Henry was a dream come true for him.

At night when we watched "the telly," we'd meet eyes and point to Henry, who slept on a little pillow on the floor by the fireplace. We'd share a smile and say, "Awwww." There was a genuine softening of both of our hearts, and I think that having a dog early on in our marriage helped strengthen our relationship.

Henry also helped me make friends in England. It wasn't as if people weren't kind in that northern coastal village, but they were reserved and I felt a bit out of place. My enthusiasm, my accent, and my ideas stood out and uncomfortably so. I dialed my personality down several notches and didn't feel much like myself. But when Henry was with me on a walk, we met all sorts of people.

They didn't talk to me as much as through Henry—"Oh it's a nice day out, isn't it?" they'd coo to him, not making eye contact with me. And I'd respond the same way, through the dog. "Yes, it's a very nice day. A bit brisk, but invigorating, I'd say." And it would go on like that for a few more exchanges, and Henry never knew he was the interlocutor.

Henry helped me come out of my shell and meet a few of the villagers, and soon we were a recognized pair and were waved to by the greengrocer, the baker, and the traffic wardens. I'm sure they were saying to each other, "There goes that beautiful dog and that crazy American woman with the Dole-Kemp T-shirt."

Though we shared this great love for Henry, Peter thought I was a bit overboard. After we moved to San Diego in January 1999 and I was working at an office while Peter started his business from his computer in our apartment, something changed. Suddenly, Henry was with Peter for most of the hours of the day, and that's when the tide turned and Peter became a bit obsessed with Henry, too. He said he was "besotted" and would even tear up when he talked about how much that dog meant to him. They were together so much that after we'd lived there awhile, when I was out on my own with Henry, once a guy in a shop said, "Oh, is that Peter's dog?" Harrumph!

Peter was a good dog trainer, too. While I helped Henry learn tricks, Peter handled the more difficult task of teaching Henry to heel while on a walk, which makes for a more pleasant experience without all of the pulling of a leash. In fact, Henry got so good at it, we almost never needed a leash for him.

Peter also took him on runs in the California sunshine, saying, "Only dogs and mad Englishmen go out in the midday sun," a play on a British expression. He thought Henry loved those outings, but years later in Washington, D.C.,

Majestic Henry in the surf in Kennebunkport, Maine, just down the road from Walker's Point.

when Peter was putting on his running shoes, he couldn't find Henry in our Capitol Hill townhouse. He looked everywhere and called and called for him. But no dog. Panicking a little, Peter started looking in every room, even in the basement. He finally found him down there, hiding in the storage room. He didn't want to go on long runs anymore. It was so endearing that Peter could barely stand it. The only thing Henry had to run after that was errands with us on the weekends.

As responsible dog owners, we agreed that Henry wouldn't be allowed on the furniture. We stuck to the rule. But then one day I came out of the shower and Henry was sleeping on the bed, which had white bedding and was made up perfectly. I shouted, "Just what do you think you're doing?" Peter ran in. Henry opened one eye and arched his brow but otherwise didn't move. We started giggling, and I relented.

"He just wants to be comfortable, too," I said. There went the "no dogs on the furniture" rule. (As a household rule enforcer, I'm less Supreme Court and more European Union.)

Not long after that, we left Henry in the apartment to go out to dinner. I used to leave the TV on for him and would often turn the channel to Animal Planet, just for kicks. At this point, Henry still wasn't supposed to be on the couch. He had a perfectly good dog bed on the floor.

When we came home a couple of hours later, the TV was blaring in Spanish. We could hear it from two flights below. Since we lived in an apartment, we were super-conscientious about not being noisy neighbors. Peter bounded up the steps and opened the door. Henry had just hopped off the couch—we could tell because the cushion was warm—and the TV was tuned to Univision.

Henry had obviously gotten up on the sofa and rolled over onto the remote and accidentally turned up the volume and changed the channel (either that or, like most North American males, he secretly enjoyed *Sábado Gigante*). We still laugh about how he must have panicked and thought, "How do you turn this thing down?!"

From then on, we pretty much let him get on any furniture he wanted, though he would always ask permission before he jumped up.

After two years in San Diego, we scraped together enough for a down payment for a small house on a canyon in a neighborhood called South Park. It was a tiny place, but it had a big deck in the back and we spent a lot of time there. It was Henry's favorite spot.

One day he saw his first lizard on the one palm tree out back. He was a dog obsessed. He'd stand there all day waiting for it to reappear. Peter worked from home and would go out and move the umbrella every hour to keep him in the shade. I worried Henry would cook out there.

Next to us was an open space where Peter and I would take Henry to exercise. We would throw rocks down into the canyon and he would scamper down to fetch them and then charge back up. He'd do this over and over until we decided he'd had enough.

On September 11, 2001, Peter made my tea and woke me so that I could get ready for work. He took Henry over to that canyon around 5:40 a.m. (Yes, we'd made Henry a "morning dog.") I got up and, still sleepy, turned on the television to watch the morning news. The first of the Twin Towers had already been attacked. As my eyes and ears adjusted to the news, I saw the second plane hit the second tower. I ran outside yelling for Peter to come back.

"They're attacking the World Trade Center with planes! Hurry!" I said. Like many, he thought I meant that a small plane had wandered off course and accidentally crashed into the building. If only that had been true.

Reports of attacks in Washington, D.C., started coming into the stations. Some of them were false; others, unfortunately, were not. I prayed. I still had many friends in the nation's capital.

I sat all day with Henry watching the news. I sent an e-mail to a friend, Mindy Tucker, with whom I'd worked on the Hill and who was then the communications director for U.S. Attorney General John Ashcroft. They were under terrorist threat and pressure—to figure out how the attacks had been planned and carried out, and to prevent more from happening. I just wanted to make sure she was okay. She responded that she was.

A couple of days later, Mindy asked if I would be willing to move back to Washington to work at the Justice Department. I said yes and started packing before we hung up the phone.

I felt sad for Henry because San Diego was such a great place to be a dog (California is a great place to be anything, except a taxpayer). The weather, the dog beaches, the laid-back friendliness of the people there, many of whom loved dogs. But there was never a question of whether we'd return to D.C., especially after the terrorist attacks. And going back to join the Bush administration changed the trajectory of my career completely. Henry was contentedly along for the ride.

I left for D.C. a couple of weeks later and Peter wrapped up our affairs in San Diego. He and Henry drove across the country, stopping to see friends along the way. Henry was a good travel companion, always there for company but not talking very much.

As Vizslas age, their faces turn white. Like Henry's here. Dogs get sweeter as they get older.

Over the years, Henry lived in Scotland, California, Washington, D.C., and New York City. He traveled across the country and visited over thirty states. He was my dog while I worked in the White House, and even the president knew him. One of my fondest memories was Henry joining the press briefing in Kennebunkport, Maine, which we held at the Colony Hotel down the road from the Bushes' family compound on Walker's Point. Henry just laid down next to the podium while I bantered with the reporters. It was a White House Press Briefing First. Henry and I liked to make history. (I was actually hoping he'd have another historic first on one particular reporter's shoes…you know who you are!)

Henry even weighed in on politics. I taught him some political tricks; for example, Henry would bark when asked if Bill Clinton should be in jail (the trigger word was "jail," so you could slot anyone's name in there and the trick worked—it came in handy years later when the star NFL quarterback Michael Vick was found guilty of cruelty to animals).

Henry could also play dead when asked about Al Gore's "lock box." I'd ask him, "So what do you think of Gore's Social Security plan?" And I would raise my eyebrows, which was Henry's signal to lie down. Anticipating a treat, Henry would often do the quickest of deaths. I wouldn't let him up until he played "all the way dead." It was great fun to show him off at parties (at least the ones with lots of Republicans in attendance and after a few cocktails).

I served for seven and a half years in the Bush administration, and Henry was with us all the time. Whereas Peter knew how stressed I was, Henry had no idea. That meant that he didn't give me a wide berth when I was on edge, as Peter would sometimes wisely do.

Henry just loved me and wanted to play when I got home. Then he'd settle down and we'd have dinner. I used to give him about half of my plate. I shouldn't have done it, but I didn't have much of an appetite given that my mind was on work most of the time. In those years when I didn't have much time for exercise, Henry helped me keep my weight down. He was like my personal Weight Watchers counselor.

Henry hated to hear any curse words, especially the "F" word. He was sensitive to vulgarity and conflict. Once we had a friend with us on a drive out to Annapolis and she was telling us a really funny story; the thing is, she can talk like a sailor, which cracks me up, but it was upsetting Henry in the backseat. I had to stop her midtale and ask her to keep it PG. She laughed but complied with my request. As soon as she did, Henry perked right back up and seemed to enjoy her story as much as we did.

He also didn't like to be teased. He'd bark his head off at us if we said, "Henry, do you have fleas?" When we'd sing Henry Vizsla to the tune of "Hare Krishna" and clap our hands, he'd bark at us like, "Stop! I'll never get that song out of my head!"

Even before social media really took off, I was known around the office as being a dog lover. Peter complained that on my bulletin board in my

Henry was a truly regal dog.

office in the White House I had more pictures of Henry than of him—but I reminded him: Who takes most of the pictures? The answer: Peter!

I was overboard with Henry, it's true. And that became more than clear one day in Crawford, Texas.

The press office was always on duty during the White House years, and when President Bush was working from his ranch, we would hold the daily press briefings at the middle school in Crawford.

I was the deputy press secretary at this point, and I was on deck to do the briefing that day. I hadn't briefed the press on camera very often, and I was really nervous. To prepare, I asked a young intern if she would pepper me with possible questions I'd written up that I might get asked in the briefing. As I drove, she prepared me.

Along the way, I went off on a tangent and was telling her a story about something that had happened the week before when I was home.

About halfway through my story she stopped me.

"Wait a second. Henry is your *dog*? All this time, I thought Henry was your *husband* and that *Peter* was your dog!" she said.

I almost had to pull over I was laughing so hard. I love both my husband and my dog, but I don't think they're interchangeable! (I just have to remind myself: Peter is the one that tells the jokes, and the dog is the one that sleeps next to me in bed...)

While Henry never got to come to the White House to play with the president's dogs, Barney and Miss Beazley, he was the talk of many meetings.

President Bush and Vice President Cheney would ask me about Henry, and they got a kick out of Henry's political tricks (especially when I'd ask Henry what he really thought of John Kerry and he'd go fetch one of my old flip-flops).

So even back in the White House days, dogs helped me connect with my colleagues—we didn't always have to talk about terror threats or tax reform some-times we just shot the breeze about our kids and our dogs.

Henry loved ice cream. Once he was older, I let him have what he wanted.

Peter Gets Arrested—Because of the Dog

(AS TOLD BY PETER)

IT'S ALL HENRY'S FAULT! My brush with the law started around 7:15 p.m. on November 15, 2007, when I took Henry to Lincoln Park. I parked across the road and was walking in the park with him; the park was deserted apart from a few other dog owners there, and we chatted about our dogs as the darkness settled around us.

We were standing near the Lincoln statue when we noticed headlights entering the park toward the far end, and we saw a police car racing down the middle of the park toward us.

We soon realized the reason for the rapid approach: It was the Park Police and our dogs were off leash. Everyone immediately called their dog and reached in their pockets for their leash. I did the same, but alas—no leash! I had left it on the seat of the car.

I quickly turned away and, with Henry walking extremely close, started to leave the park.

"You! Stop!" I heard. I turned and sure enough, the policeman had leapt from his car and was advancing rapidly toward me. Busted!

I explained to Officer Smith that I had left my leash in the car and was returning for it, so he asked for ID, then instructed me to wait while he went to the car. He took a few minutes, presumably checking I was not a serial dog-off-leash scofflaw and returned to write the ticket.

I tried to make light of the situation and joke with Officer Smith, but he was all business. No response, no smile, no pleasantries in reply to mine.

I duly received my ticket and was told that I could pay at any of the stations listed on the back. I informed Officer Smith that there were some suspicious squirrels at the end of the park that he might want to check on, and returned to my car.

Okay, I got a ticket. I was in the wrong, I broke the law and I am not arguing with that. I had fifteen days in which to pay and so on November 24 I reported to First District Substation on E Street SE in Washington, D.C., as listed on the back of the ticket.

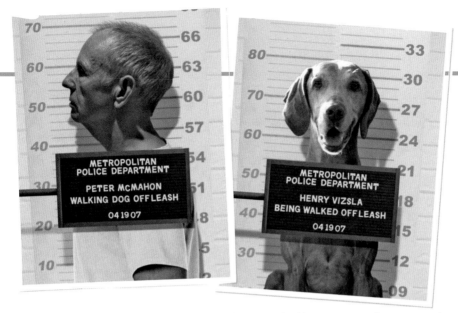

I was informed that they did not accept the payments anymore, and my inquiry as to where they thought I might be able to pay was met with a disinterested shrug and the words "Park Police headquarters."

I returned home and, as we were leaving town for a couple of days, I decided to call the Park Police headquarters on Ohio Drive SW to check whether they accepted payment, or ask where I should mail the check, as the ticket stated, "You may mail in the collateral" but did not state where to mail the payment, how to make the payment, or to whom the payment should be made. However, all I got was an answering machine; an hour later I got the same. Are you starting to see a pattern here?

I have since learned that the ticket I received with both wrong and missing information had been incorrect for six years. A friend got a ticket six years prior and the station on E Street SE did not accept payment then.

So I duly wrote a check made out to U.S. Park Police and mailed it to the headquarters, with a letter explaining that their ticket contained wrong and insufficient information. I also stated, "I know that the job of ticketing dog owners whose dog is off leash is highly important—especially in time of war and terror threats, not to mention D.C.'s soaring crime rate. However, if someone at your department could see their way to having a ticket written in competent language with correct information, perhaps we might feel our taxes are not being totally squandered."

They received my letter and did not reply for twelve days before stating that my payment was unacceptable and that I should send a money order to the D.C. Court.

By the time I received the letter it was already ten days past the cutoff date and the ticket stated that this would "result in the case being presented at the District of Columbia Superior Court for disposition."

Given that I had made three attempts to pay, and some information on the ticket lacked sufficient details while other information was just plain wrong, I decided to have my day in court. I wanted to explain to the judge just how apathetic/indolent/incompetent the Park Police are with their tickets. And as a newly minted citizen (for all of about two months), I knew it was my right!

I was therefore awaiting notice to attend court, but did not hear anything for some time. Given that the Park Police are apparently incapable of producing a competently written ticket, this didn't surprise me. However, upon returning from a business trip in April I found a letter inviting me to go to the police station on Fourth Street SW so that they could process me through court on the same day. This was part of "Operation Clean Slate." (I'm not kidding or exaggerating.)

On Wednesday the eighteenth I went to the station but was told it was too late for processing that day and was asked to return early the next morning, preferably before 7 a.m. When I asked how long the process would be, I was told, "Oh, an hour and a half, maybe two hours."

So on the nineteenth I arrived at the station at 6:45 a.m. and was promptly arrested! The arresting officer asked what had happened and he shook his head in amazement. "They issued a warrant for that?" he asked incredulously. "Why didn't you go to the court and pay the fine?"

Oops! That's something else not mentioned on the ticket . . . Apparently the Park Police expect citizens to be psychic. So during the twelve days my letter was sitting in the Park Police headquarters being ignored, they had gone ahead and issued a warrant.

My belongings and belt were taken and I was placed in a cell. Now, I am a normal, law-abiding person. I've never been in a cell in my life, and my reaction was somewhere between surprise and fascination. It was just like the TV shows. The fact that I knew a judge would release me as soon as I was through the court proceeding meant that I was never worried—this was in no way a long-term situation—but it was strange to know that I could not leave if I wanted to. I no longer had any control over my own freedom and while awaiting transportation to the court I contemplated how awful it must be for someone who knows they will be incarcerated for a long time. It doesn't matter how many times you see it on the TV; it's different when you are there yourself. I was tempted to ask if I could get a tattoo of Henry on my shoulder to mark the occasion.

However, when the other prisoners were taken to court and I remained there, I inquired as to why and was told that, as I was a Park Police case, I must await a Park Police officer.

Of course nobody turned up from the Park Police station for a couple of hours, so I sat and waited patiently, counting the tiles on the floor (8,280) and finding the whole situation actually quite amusing. Though by this time I knew that the parking meter was running out for my car; so much for a couple of hours.

Finally, the Park Police arrived and it was none other than my old nemesis Officer Smith! He searched me again and, after handcuffing me, led me to his car. At least I sat in the front so it wouldn't look like I had been arrested if anyone I knew saw me.

When he got into the driver's seat, I said, "When you put me in the car, weren't you supposed to put your hand on my head, like they do in the movies?" He did not respond.

I tried making conversation with Officer Smith but the responses were monosyllabic and usually one word. I tried making jokes, but they fell on deaf ears. All business, this guy (or maybe the squirrel jibe was still rankling him). Upon arrival at the headquarters building, I was taken to another cell and the cuffs were released, then after five minutes Officer Smith brought me out and cuffed me to a wooden bar while he filled in the necessary paperwork. It's probably just as well he did, because by this time I was considering fleeing. If I could just overpower this young, fit, armed officer and steal his ID to open the door before anyone noticed—the place was after all virtually empty—I could be free! I could see the headlines: **LEASHLESS DOG WALKER STALKS D.C. PARKS**.

I knew I was also allowed to call my wife, but I was a little afraid to. Dana had

The Washington Post

Leashless Dog Walker Stalks DC Parks

Man escapes police custody, still at large

warned me several times about getting that ticket paid, and when I told her I was going to exercise my rights she told me I was going to be arrested. I didn't believe her. Now I was going to have to call her at the White House where she was the acting press secretary and surely "didn't need this crap." Her White House voice can still scare me to this day.

So I said to Officer Smith that I would like to make a call. He looked at me blankly.

"I've seen the movies. I know my rights," I said with a smile.

He grudgingly obliged.

When I called the press office, her assistant press secretary Carlton Carroll answered the phone. He said she was in the Oval Office and asked if I wanted to interrupt the meeting. Over my dead body! So I asked him to leave her a message, which he promptly e-mailed. She saw a message came in and snuck a peek at her Blackberry. All it said was that I had been delayed and that she needed to arrange for the dog walker to come take care of Henry.

She later told me that she knew immediately. "That jerk's been arrested." (Right on both counts.)

More handcuffs, another car, and I was soon at the court building, where, once Officer Smith was sure we were behind locked doors, I was handed over to the processing officers.

Form-filling and fingerprinting followed; however, these fellows, while highly professional, were a lot more relaxed. When they asked the reason for my arrest and I told them "walking my dog without a leash," the response was hilarity. I think I was the first, as it took them some time to find the nearest category for me on the computer!

When they stopped laughing, a mature officer of some years' service also told me, "This is ridiculous." He explained that most officers would have used their initiative, had the warrant delayed for a couple of days, and made a call, or even visited me to tell me to go to the court and pay.

Still we enjoyed the humor of the situation and made a few wisecracks, while they fed me cheese sandwiches and lemonade and, after ten minutes in my third cell, I was cuffed again and placed in the back of yet another car to be taken to the Superior Court building a couple of hundred yards away.

By this time, it was early afternoon, and the officer driving told us he was rushing so that we would be processed that afternoon. He explained that if we weren't processed that day it would mean an overnight stay. Now it wasn't quite so funny!

When he asked the reason for my arrest and I told him, it resulted in the same outburst of disbelieving laughter. "Are you serious? You were arrested for that?"

So now I arrived at the Superior Court, where the handcuffs were finally removed, only to be replaced with leg shackles! "If my friends could only see me now," I thought with a wry smile.

Following another search, I found myself in the fourth cell, one I shared with twenty others.

A couple hours more cell time and after three court-appointed attorneys shared the humor of the situation and expressed their disbelief that an arrest had been made for this, I found myself in front of the judge.

I explained what had happened and even the judge smiled. With my English accent I was clearly a relative newcomer to the United States, and I had made three attempts to pay via a Park Police system that I described to him as blatantly incompetent, but it had not been possible given the inadequate information they provided.

The judge told me that this should not have happened and that I should not have been there that day. I held up my manacled leg and said, "Well, Your Honor, it's been a very interesting day and I've had a good insight into the U.S. judicial system." He smiled and said, "Welcome to America!"

Upon payment my record would be expunged, and I left the court a free man. I had to collect my belongings from the Park Police station the next day—they had told me that after 3 p.m. the office would be closed. I hope nobody went there to pay a fine that afternoon.

As my car keys were with the belongings, I walked there with Henry on a delightful April morning. (On the leash all the way, I would add! Well, most of it . . .)

Oh, and the good news was. . . I did not get a parking ticket after being off the meter all the previous day! But if I had, I would have paid that ticket right away. 🐾

One Last Swim

Henry loved to swim. So much.
CREDIT: J. DAVID AKE

Henry was an athletic dog but had a few health problems along the way. He used to dive underwater for big rocks, stay under while he hunted for the right one, and then bring it to the surface, his tail up and proud. Unfortunately, this led him to crack one of his molars and he had to have major dental surgery.

He also had several cysts that had to be removed over the years, and some of those had precancerous cells. But it was in his thirteenth year that he really started to fade. The diagnosis was Cushing's disease.

There was really nothing more they could do.

Vizslas go gray early, starting around five or six, and when I used to worry that Henry wasn't well or that he was aging too quickly, Peter would point to his own head and say, "He looks just like me. Distinguished." By the time Vizslas are ten, many of them have gone mostly white in the face, which makes me love them even more.

When I started work on *The Five* and we planned to move to New York, I fretted about Henry's health. I knew that taking him out of his home and his neighborhood was going to be stressful.

Peter assured me he would be taking care of Henry and that I didn't need to worry. They got to know everyone in the neighborhood—they'd stop and play Trivial Pursuit with the doormen in our building, get an ice

Henry was an early fan of The Five.

cream from Scotty on Forty-Fourth Street, and have a chat with the guy that sold vintage comic books on the corner. It seemed like everyone in Midtown knew Mr. Henry.

Sadly, I was right about the move being hardest for our dog. The city was loud and chaotic. There was no grass or trees in our area. Henry had to ride in an elevator just to go outside to do his business on noisy Forty-Second Street. (Henry relieving himself on the busiest block in the center of the Western world is a metaphor for something…I'm just not sure what.)

Henry's world was upended and his health started to fail just as my new career was taking off. I wanted to enjoy that new job fully, but my mind was often on the dog I'd loved for so long.

It's been a few years since that time, and yet I still have difficulty telling this story without crying. And I know that my fellow dog owners will understand exactly how I feel.

With every dog story, there's a joyful beginning, a wonderful, charming middle, and a tearful end.

Here's what happened. I knew Henry was not doing well and didn't think he'd live through the summer. It was March 2012, and the weather was starting to show some signs of a thaw. I wanted to take Henry to his favorite place—the beach. We finally found a dog-friendly beach online and planned to go that weekend.

Traffic in the city is always terrible, and I'm a nervous passenger. I was worried sick about Henry and my energy was spent from a long week of work where we'd argued about the presidential election on every show. When a driver cut us off, I snapped at Peter and he snapped back at me, and Henry shrank back into the seat. Then I felt even worse. We just needed to get to the beach. We drove in silence.

When we got there, the beach was a long distance from the parking lot. And there were big signs saying, DOGS MUST BE LEASHED AT ALL TIMES. Some dog beach that was.

Henry struggled on the soft sand on the way there, so we took it easy. The wind was strong. When we finally got to the beach, Henry smelled the salt air and he got a little pep in his step. I took off his leash. There weren't many people around and I couldn't imagine anyone would hassle us for letting our geriatric dog have one last romp in the waves. He even trotted a bit into the water.

Peter and I met eyes. We were both crying, but this time not because he was so cute, but because we knew he was going to leave us soon.

"See how happy he is," Peter said.

It was so windy we couldn't carry on a conversation. But I felt the fresh air was doing us all some good. When we started the long walk back up the beach, Henry faltered and his front legs buckled. I yelped. Peter scrambled in the sand to help him up.

Henry couldn't walk, so Peter picked up our seventy-five-pound dog and carried him for a while. Eventually, Peter set him back down on the sand, and Henry was able to walk very slowly back to the car.

Peter and I were barely speaking—no longer because of our anger from earlier in the day, but out of fear and worry.

On the ride home, I held Henry's chin in my hand and we agreed—something was very wrong.

We had painkillers for Henry and we gave him one. (I considered taking one myself.) By the time we got back to the apartment, Henry still seemed to be in pain, so we gave him another pill. But that just made him seem drunk. Henry wasn't at all himself.

A few hours later with no improvement, Peter decided he had to take him to the emergency vet on Fifty-Fifth Street. He hurried to get dressed for the winter night, and I kissed Henry on the head and told Peter to hurry.

I didn't go with him. And that's one of the biggest regrets of my life.

Because Henry never came home.

The next morning, we hoped to go pick him up. But the call we got was that we needed to get to the hospital immediately. Henry was fading.

The taxi driver must have thought the world was ending. In many ways, ours was. We managed to tell him where we needed to go.

English wasn't our driver's first language, and usually Peter talks to taxi drivers and often he's been to their home countries. We felt terrible that we seemed so rude since we were so distraught. When he pulled up to the curb outside of the Blue Pearl Animal Hospital, he turned to us and kindly said, "I am so sorry." I wish I could have hugged him, but we were running out of time.

When we got there, we were ushered downstairs into the ICU-type room. There were lots of other pets there—including a rabbit, and I remember thinking, "Who has a rabbit in NYC?" (My friend later told me the answer: French chefs.)

Henry was on the floor hooked up to an oxygen machine. I got on my knees and kissed his face and thanked him for being such a good dog. Peter could barely manage to do the same.

I stood and remembered what my grandfather, who had such a soft spot for animals, told me on the ranch. "Never ever let an animal suffer."

"Doctor, we're okay. We're ready," I said.

I led Peter out of the unit and into the private room where the vet explained he would bring Henry in and administer the shot. Those moments were unbearable. Through tears I e-mailed my mom and my sister, who were in shock in Denver. They didn't know Henry was so ill.

My grief was compounded by watching Peter. My husband was collapsing inside. His face was nearly unrecognizable, and I never want to see that again.

A few moments later the doctor came in, but Henry wasn't with him.

"As soon as you left the room, Henry passed away. It's as if he was waiting for your permission to go," the doctor said.

We sobbed.

Oh, Henry. I believe he stayed alive long enough for us to say good-bye.

What a gentleman . . . No, what a dog.

We slowly walked back to the apartment. It was a really cold day. As we approached the building, the doorman and building staff were there, expecting news on Henry. All we could do was shrug and look up, our faces wet with tears.

"Oh no. We're so sorry, you guys," the doorman said, and a couple of the building staff started crying with us.

We thanked them and went up the dreaded forty-six floors to the apartment.

When the door shut, our grief took hold. I'm talking full-on meltdown for the entire day. It was March 25, 2012.

As the night wore on, I put away the sneakers I'd worn to the beach with Henry the day before. They still had sand in them. They still do, in fact. I keep them in the back of my closet. I can't bear to throw them away.

Peter managed to get a note written that he sent to our friends and family, and we got lots of calls and messages because they knew how much Henry meant to us.

Still, neither of us stopped crying for hours . . . days . . . I wasn't able to get ahold of myself.

It wasn't until writing this that I could look back and thought about why.

When I first picked up Henry in Scotland, I was twenty-six years old and had just made a major life decision to leave the United States and my great job on Capitol Hill to move to England to be with the man I fell in love with on a plane.

My head was a bit in the clouds—I was fairly carefree but becoming a woman. I didn't have much responsibility, and I spent my days learning about the UK and reading novels for hours at a time.

Two months later, I got married at the justice of the peace in England and honeymooned in Santorini. I immediately felt different about my relationship with Peter—he went from being my serious boyfriend to being my family.

And Henry gave us such joy. I was in love and loved. It was a happy, easy time.

Over the next fourteen years, my life would change in many ways.

We moved to San Diego where I tried to fit into the public relations culture there, but that career track didn't stick. I missed Washington, and after 9/11 I had the opportunity to return and work for the Bush administration at the Department of Justice.

Soon after I started at Justice, I got pulled over to the White House, where I would meet another man that eventually would change my life forever: President George W. Bush, who eventually chose me as his press secretary.

My seven years of service in the administration took a physical and emotional toll on me, mostly because of the hours and the intensity of the stress of the work.

Of course, becoming the White House press secretary was the best thing that ever happened to my career. I learned so much—about policy, world affairs, management, and politics.

But the most important lesson I learned working for President Bush was about character and how to conduct myself under stress and attack. I found out how to be productive despite obstacles, and appreciated how a communicator can help calm a situation, advance a negotiation, or lead to a solution.

The press secretary is the pinnacle for a public relations professional—it was the opportunity of a lifetime.

But having worked in politics for so many years, I'd built up a fairly tough exterior. The daily battles can wear a person out, and in some ways, I became edgier and harder than I'd ever been.

It was also a lofty position, and the surest way you can lose your way in Washington, D.C., is to let any of that power or prestige go to your head.

Throughout those years, Henry kept me from losing sight of what was important in life: appreciation and gratitude for my health and blessings, and the love I shared with Peter and our dog.

We were a unit—the three of us stuck together. We knew each other better than anyone else in the world. As Harry Truman once said, "If you want a friend in Washington, get a dog." And as Charles Krauthammer suggests, get two—in case the first one turns on you.

What I learned at the White House served me well when I went on and transitioned from being the spokesperson for the Leader of the Free

World to speaking for myself. I'd never said in public what my personal opinions were before I joined Fox News as a contributor—and while it is somewhat freeing to do so, it is a bit like walking on a high wire without a net. And it doesn't come without a price. The criticism from an increasingly unhinged social media network can be withering, and it takes a thick skin, a strong stomach, and a humble sense of humor to manage it.

And through it all, there were Peter and Henry.

While Peter mostly understood what I was going through, Henry had no idea.

He didn't know that I'd yelled at a reporter or was sick to my stomach thinking about an article that I knew would hit the next morning.

He didn't know that I was juggling too many balls and constantly lived in worry that I was going to drop one and that the consequences would be severe.

When I would lie awake at night thinking through all the things I could have said or should have done, he'd lie next to our bed and snore lightly—which wasn't annoying; it actually made me smile. In contrast, if Peter snored, he got pushed to roll over.

Henry didn't care that I got to dine in the State Dining Room with heads of state, celebrities, and some of the most interesting and accomplished people in the world.

He didn't know about my sharp tongue and my occasional atomic elbow that I used to help get me through the job.

Henry knew me just as his mom. He made me look forward to getting picked up after work, because he'd be sitting on the backseat and he'd put his chin on my shoulder as we rode home.

Peter would ask me, "How was your day?" but I wouldn't be ready to relive it yet, so I'd say, "Can I hear about your and Henry's day first?"

And then Peter would tell me all about what Henry had done, because he knew that was what I most wanted to hear.

Henry made me get outside for fresh air, to take walks through our

Capitol Hill neighborhood; we'd stroll to the coffee shop where they'd give him a biscuit and go to Frager's hardware store to have a look around the garden shop.

He kept me grounded in the heady life I had at the White House and in New York City working in television.

Henry was a witness to my transition from the young woman of twenty-six to the more confident woman of nearly forty. So much in my life had changed in those fourteen years, but Henry was the constant for Peter and me. I didn't know who I would have been without him.

Henry's final autumn. Peter took this picture in Annapolis, right before we moved to New York City. We were excited by the new opportunity but worried about the toll it would take on Henry.

Around 10 p.m. the night Henry died, my phone rang. I couldn't imagine who was calling so late and worried it was more bad news.

But it was our friend and fellow dog lover, Greta Van Susteren of Fox News.

"Dana, I know the last thing you think you should do right now is get another puppy, but I'm telling you it's the best way to heal your heart," Greta said.

Greta has a contagious confidence. She really makes you feel like you can do something—and she has strong opinions and very good advice.

I told her all the reasons I thought I couldn't get another dog while living in New York City, but she insisted we think about it.

I told Peter about the call, but he said we couldn't replace Henry.

Two nights later, at a diner we went to because the apartment was too silent, we looked at each other and said, "We can do this."

Greta was right.

So that night, finally showing some signs of life after the death of Henry, we fell in love with our new puppy that we'd never even met.

We even named him: Jasper.

Nicknames

Every dog has its proper name and also several nicknames. It's inevitable—if you've ever had a dog, you know what I mean. The funny thing is, they answer to all of them.

NICKNAMES FOR HENRY:

Mr. Henry

Mr. H

H

Hank

Poo (as in the Mr. Hankey, the Christmas Poo from *South Park*)

Poo Bear

Boo

Kangaroo

Turkey Legs

King Henry

Henry Krishna (For kicks, we'd sing "Henry Krishna" and clap our hands, and he'd bark his head off.)

Goose (the silly variety)

FiveFan Photoshops gave me this wonderful gift. This is what Henry and Jasper would look like if they'd had a chance to stand side by side.

NICKNAMES FOR JASPER:

Sir Jasper	Pumpkinhead	Chicken	J-Man
Jaspy	Peanut	Noodle	Mr. J
Jasperino	Lil' Ear	Baby	Monster
Jasperpoo			

Jasper

Why the name Jasper?

Well, it sounded like a proper British name. A good one to follow our distinguished Henry.

Peter had a friend in England who used to say, "Well, would you look at the size of that Jasper!" when he saw something interesting. It made me smile.

Besides, we think "Jasper" is a fun word to say. When you're naming a dog, you have to test it out. Imagine you're at the dog park and you're trying to get your dog's attention—what name do you want to yell out loud for all the world to hear?

One of our friends learned this lesson in a cute way. After months of lobbying by their young kids to get a dog, they finally caved. That was good. But then they let the kids name him. And guess what they came up with? Cuddles. Now the dad, who had dog walking duty, couldn't imagine being at the dog park yelling, "Cuddles! Cuddles, come back!" So he nicknamed him Mr. C—a good compromise that preserved his neighborhood street cred.

Thankfully, Jasper was a name that fit the dog (and that Peter felt was appropriately masculine enough). Or Jasper fit the name. Anyway, it worked.

When we decided to get a puppy after Henry died, we were fortunate that a Vizsla breeder we knew from the D.C. area had just had a new litter. Henry used to stay at this breeder's farm when we had to be away. He loved it. There were no kennels, just acres of leash-free fun and sleeping on the bed, not in a crate. The breeder knew the kind of dog owners we were and said she'd choose the right puppy for us.

Jasper was born on April 9, 2012, and we had to wait until early June to pick him up. The gap between those two months was never ending to us.

Jasper was so small, I used a $20 bill to show his size. Priceless.

Our apartment was silent without Henry, and we didn't leave for hours at a time because there was no dog to take down for a little wander. We went on a couple of long weekend vacations to try to pass the time; one to the beautiful resort at Sea Island, Georgia, where instead of relaxing on the beach or kayaking in the river, we cried our eyes out about Henry. I felt sorry for the waitstaff; we'd take pains to explain to them we weren't crying over the filet mignon. They were kind; we left big tips.

Another weekend we went upstate to Mohonk Mountain House and instead of enjoying the hiking, we kept thinking about how much Henry would have loved it.

We weren't completely lost, though. Because we spent a lot of our time talking about our dog-to-be. That made us happy.

As the date got closer, our excitement grew. We were like kids counting down to Christmas.

Finally, on June 5, we got to meet Jasper.

We pulled up to the breeder's home in a farming area of Maryland, and I dashed out of the car before it could come to a full stop. I barely said hello to the homeowners and went immediately toward the puppy pen in the living room. There were four puppies left, three females and Jasper. He was the biggest male of the litter, just as I'd requested.

"And he's the sweetest one, too," the breeder said.

She was right.

At the farm, the day we picked up Jasper. Our first photo together.

We visited with the breeders for a while and Jasper's female siblings had a fun time ganging up on him out on the back porch. We didn't want to leave but we needed to get on the road back to New York City before rush-hour traffic.

I held Jasper in my arms in the passenger seat. He was a little stiff, struggling against me like a baby that pushes away a stranger. But I had a firm hold. I wasn't going to let him go.

Since I love a fountain Diet Coke, we stopped at a drive-thru before we hit the highway.

At the window I asked the clerk, "Do you want to see my puppy?" I held him up and she gave me what I needed—confirmation that he was beautiful. (Fast-food window clerks have seen it all!)

About an hour into the journey, Jasper gave up the struggle and let me cuddle him. I kept kissing his head.

And then I noticed something strange about his left ear. I looked at his right ear and then back to the left. I wondered if my eyes were playing tricks, but no. It was definitely shorter, and it looked like it had been cut into an arc somehow, like with a pizza cutter.

"Peter, did you see this?" I asked. He hadn't noticed—probably because I hadn't let him hold Jasper yet.

I called the breeder and asked if something was wrong with Jasper. She said she hadn't noticed either, and with nine puppies to look after maybe that was true. But it was really obvious that he had one ear smaller than the other.

We never planned to show him, so that wasn't a problem for us. It was just so strange, and I worried about how it had happened and if it had hurt. (Years later, a fan sent me a photo of Jasper at four weeks old. She had chosen one of Jasper's littermates for her new pet. In the picture, you can clearly see his left ear is shorter than the other. That was another example of connecting to a new friend on social media.)

The day we brought Jasper home. It wasn't until we'd had him for a couple of hours that I noticed that his left ear was smaller than his right.

But as with most unique attributes, Jasper's mismatched ear eventually became his most endearing trait. He has no idea why we call him "Li'l Ear" or laugh when his ears flop inside out and one is so much longer than the other. When we take a photograph of him from behind, I love to see his lopsided head. He's so perfect and symmetrical in every other way that the little ear rounds him out nicely. It gives him character.

Happy and secure puppies love to lie on their backs. Stuffed elephants too.

The drive took about three hours. Jasper was unimpressed with the New York City skyline, but Peter and I never tire of it.

As you can imagine, Manhattan was a shock to our farm puppy. The first thing that went by us on the street was a screaming ambulance, the second a Harley-Davidson, followed by a stream of yellow taxis with honking horns. The noise followed us up to our living room.

Jasper was spooked and ran behind my legs. I picked him up and calmed him. He got used to the noises pretty quickly, and now he doesn't pay any mind to the sirens on the streets (but sometimes I still cover his ears). He seems not to mind the sounds of dropped garbage cans and construction trucks at 5 a.m. I wish I had his ability to tune it out.

After introducing him to the doormen, we went up the elevator to our apartment. I set him down and showed him his first toy, a little yellow giraffe. It was so sweet.

But only for a second. Because in the next moment, he looked at me with his dark blue eyes and peed on the rug.

"No, no, no!" I cried, and tried to take him over to the puppy papers.

He ignored those and soon peed again on the rug.

This was unacceptable—even in New York City.

I realized he had no idea what potty training meant, whereas Henry had been so easy to train fourteen years ago. Henry had only a handful of accidents in the house, and that was only when he was playing so hard he lost track of himself. I tried not to compare Jasper to Henry, but it was difficult not to. I sensed a long road ahead with more than a little dread.

Peter and I had a lot of discussions about how we'd manage to train Jasper in a high-rise. Peter promised me he would never complain about having to take him down to the street level to do his business, and he never did. But it was difficult.

We had about fifty yards from our apartment to the elevator. It took a while for the elevators to come. When they did, the car usually had to stop five to seven times before it got to the lobby. Then we had to get through the lobby and out to the street, avoiding people and taxis, before the puppy could pee. Now that's a lot to ask of anyone, let alone a two-month-old puppy. You should've seen how I would scramble up to the apartment some days when I'd walked home from the studio. Yikes!

We tried all sorts of things to trick Jasper into holding it until we got outside. Peter would keep his mind off it by racing him down the hallway to the elevator, stopping often to tell him to sit, because we were told he wouldn't pee if he was sitting.

That isn't true. Jasper would sit and then a big fountain of pee would start (and that's impossible to stop!). We were forever in the hallway trying to clean up the stains.

Jasper got to the point that he didn't want to go into the hall because that's where he got in trouble for peeing on the carpet. So then he wouldn't pee in the apartment, but he didn't want to leave, either. So we had to coax him out. We tried everything—food, squeaky toys, pleading, tickets to the opera…Often we had to give up and just carry him because we didn't have time for tricks and games before he'd need to go.

One of my sweetest memories was watching Jasper hold on to his dad's neck with his two paws and rest his chin on his shoulder as he was carried into the hall and down to the lobby. (I began to think that Peter was the potty training whisperer.) It seemed like Jasper knew he wasn't able to get it through his little puppy skull and he was embarrassed. Which made him even more endearing.

Eventually, Jasper's bladder grew enough to hold it longer so that he didn't need to be hauled over our shoulders. But then I kind of missed carrying him around.

Potty training from forty-six floors up was a lot to ask of any puppy. Peter ended up carrying Jasper, because Jasper was reluctant to go into the hallway where he often lost control of his bladder. If he was carried, there was no problem!

Once I was in a hurry and decided I'd just try to carry him. I looked ridiculous, like I was lugging a forty-pound sack of potatoes… but I loved holding him and knew I wouldn't be able to do it for much longer.

As Jasper grew, he needed more room to run. He was an active puppy. I loved how he'd make figure-eight obstacle courses for himself in the apartment, zooming from one room to the next, under the coffee table and around the rocking chair, into the bedroom and back. He ruined the loops on the handwoven rug, but we didn't mind.

We'd sit in the kitchen and watch him go back and forth,

grinning with the joy of seeing a playful puppy destroy our apartment. Peter's theory is that puppies are so cute for a reason—if they weren't, we'd kill them out of extreme frustration.

When the apartment was too small and he needed some off-leash running space, we'd go to separate ends of our apartment floor and call to him just with hand signals so we didn't disturb our neighbors, and Jasper would sprint from one end to the next, getting all of his energy out. (Later we found out that a Vizsla's top speed is even faster than a Whippet's, thirty-six to forty miles per hour, respectively. Another bragging point, yet one that's not necessarily an advantage in a New York apartment.)

There was also a doggy day care in our building. My grandfather would never have believed such a thing existed, but I think he would have approved. Heck, he may have even wanted to work there.

The doggy day care staff saved us. They'd pick up Jasper at 11 a.m. and he'd stay for the puppy and small dog hour and then again for the big dog hour. He was dropped off around 3 p.m., exhausted from all the finger painting. I kid—the dogs just wrestled for hours.

Doggy Day Care group photo on Jasper's last day before we moved to the Upper West Side to be nearer to Central Park.

They also helped us with his training, taking him outside to do his business and practicing the basics with him. The woman that ran the day care had such a strong voice that I told Peter, "If she told me to sit, I'd sit!"

There were other advantages for a puppy living in an apartment. Jasper loved to ride on the luggage carts, and the doormen would fetch one for

Jasper loved to ride on the luggage carts as a puppy.

him so that we could give him a little ride around the lobby. And they'd give him treats every time he came in from a wander around the block.

In the mornings, Peter would walk Jasper up to Central Park for its leash-free hours, and by the time he got back, he'd been gone two and a half hours. Our lease was coming due and we realized we needed to leave our apartment with a great view so that we could be closer to the park.

When we left that building, we offered to replace the carpet in the hallway, but they turned a blind eye to it.

"You're not the only one with a dog up there," the manager said with a wink.

And really, if peeing on the rug is the worst thing that happens in your New York apartment building, you got off easy.

Dog on the Loose—and Dragging a Table

(AS TOLD BY PETER)

IN THE SUMMER OF 2012, Dana was in Florida at the Republican Convention, so I decided to take four-month-old Jasper to visit friends in Annapolis. They of course loved the adorable puppy, and I took him for walks and let him swim on a small beach.

One morning I decided to take him to the City Dock area where I had often walked with Henry; he and I would stop at a small café there and sit outside—he would enjoy a biscotti while I drank my coffee.

I tied Jasper's leash to a wrought-iron table and told him to sit while I went and ordered my drink. As he was just outside the door I could see him through the glass.

Just after I turned away to pay for my drink, someone said to me, "Excuse me, is that your dog?" Thinking he was about to say the usual "cute puppy" or

Jasper on the beach. Can you tell he wants to go kayaking?

similar, I smiled, nodded, and looked out the window, at which point my smile vanished.

Jasper was running across the road dragging the table behind him.

I rushed from the coffee shop just as he was reaching the other side where a truck was parked and unloading. Jasper had moved and pulled the table—this made a noise, which frightened him, and he took off.

Unfortunately, this only exacerbated the situation, as the table was banging and clanking at the other end of the leash, and he was unable to escape the very thing he was running from.

I ran across the road shouting, "Jasper, Jasper, it's okay, baby," but by the time I reached the other side, he had run around the truck and was about to cross the road again. He might have been only four months old, but he was already strong and surprisingly fast—even pulling a table!

He then rounded the front of the truck and commenced back across the road. Fortunately, the street was quiet with no traffic, but a Mercedes and a BMW were parked diagonal to the curb, and he chose to run through the parking space between them. The dollar signs flashed before my eyes, but by a miracle he and his hitched-up table passed through leaving the vehicles unscathed.

By the time I finally caught him, he had crossed the road again on his second lap, and the table got stuck under the tail lift of the truck. The poor little guy was frantic, so I held him and talked gently to calm him. But as soon as we started back across the road, me dragging the table this time, he freaked out again, so I had to carry the table.

When I looked up I saw a gaggle of faces at the window of the café as the laughing customers all took in the spectacle. I tied Jasper to the parking meter, then went inside for my drink.

"I don't suppose anyone got that on video?"

They had not. I was partly disappointed and partly relieved because my first thought was, "Dana is going to kill me."

(I waited a couple of weeks to tell her. Thankfully, she saw the humor in it by then!) 🐾

Separation Anxiety—But Whose?

One of the things I've never been good at is teaching a dog that it is okay for them to be alone. Partly because I don't particularly like to be alone either. I project my feelings onto my dogs.

I didn't do a great job with leaving Henry by himself when we lived in England, and I did an even worse job with Jasper.

But I wasn't alone to blame—Jasper was different.

From the first week we had Jasper, I could tell that he was unlike any other dog I'd known.

Where Henry was regal, Jasper was goofy; where Henry learned tricks right away, Jasper didn't seem to grasp the idea—he'd just look at me, head tilted, as if he was saying, "I don't get it." He also may have been wondering, "Who is this crazy lady?"; and where Henry accepted that he wasn't allowed on the furniture (for the most part), Jasper never once thought he didn't belong on the bed or the couch. I wasn't too strict, though.

While Henry was affectionate, he didn't try to be on top of us all the time. He was happy to lie in his bed or on the floor in front of the fire.

Henry was dignified and would be excited but not crazed. He kept his cool.

Jasper, on the other hand, felt every emotion and showed it.

He was sillier, funnier, sadder, and more frightened than any dog I'd met. When I tried to teach him to bark on command, like I did with Henry, Jasper cowered when I pretended to bark at him (I've also tried this on Gutfeld; doesn't work).

And he was the least food-oriented dog I'd ever had, so teaching him with treats was difficult. He just wasn't interested in food, and we had to coax him to eat. He was, in many ways, like a very sensitive adolescent, without the goth eyeliner.

Henry accepted his role as the family dog, but Jasper thought he was one of us. When I stood at the kitchen counter working on my laptop, in my favorite first-position ballet pose, Jasper curled up in the triangle between my feet. If I went to the bathroom, he sat on the rug. He never took his eyes off me. I looked anywhere but at him—as you can imagine, it was a little awkward!

We intended to train Jasper to be in a crate when we were gone. It is a very good way to keep a dog safe and to teach them to be alone. And Jasper actually liked going into the crate we got him. He'd twist himself into the strangest positions and go into the crate even by himself. There was just one little thing. He didn't like the crate door to be shut, so I didn't close it.

And that's how I ruined him.

I loved to work from home getting ready for the show when Jasper was a puppy.

How could we say no to that face!?

Okay, he clearly wasn't ruined, but one day I did exactly what I'd have told others not to do.

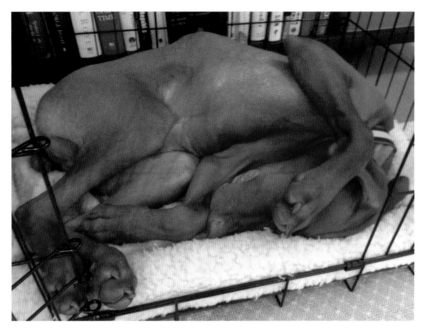

Jasper in a normal "comfy" position, sleeping in his crate. I love pliable puppies.

It was October 2012, and the presidential election between President Barack Obama and Governor Mitt Romney was intense. I was asked to appear on Governor Mike Huckabee's weekend Fox News program on a Saturday afternoon, and I agreed. The problem was Peter was out of the country on business, and Jasper hadn't been left on his own for that long before then.

I hired a young woman to come take care of him—she'd not been to the apartment before and misjudged the time it would take to get there. She was running late, and I needed to get to the studio. She promised me she would be only fifteen minutes more, so I decided that Jasper and I were going to have to part ways and I would have to leave him alone for the first time.

From an early age, Jasper had watched every move we made. He may not have been able to do all the tricks Henry could, but he was smart and intuitive. He picked up on routines quickly—shutting my laptop was his first clue that I was going out. Putting my dress and shoes into my tote bag was confirmation that I was about to leave. He'd sit in front of the coat closet so that he had to be moved to open the door. And sunglasses or keys confirmed his worst fear—that was when he knew for sure that I was about to leave. I saw panic in his eyes.

I shouldn't have been so worried, because Peter had left him alone in the apartment with the crate closed with no problems. And I was making matters worse, because Jasper was surely picking up on my nervous energy.

But Jasper and I had always had this connection. I remember when he first was taken for a walk by his dog walker, Barbara. I cried as he went down the hallway, looking back at me. I thought he'd be scared because no one besides Peter and I had ever cared for him. He wasn't, and Barbara has become one of his favorite humans.

Like a mom saying good-bye to her child on the first day of kindergarten, I was, in a word, ridiculous. I know Jasper is a dog and not a child—but he and Henry were the closest things to children that I ever took care of. And it felt good to feel that kind of love, to be protective over a beating heart. Given a chance, I'd take that emotion over any other, any time.

I knew all of this and still I had a lot of anxiety about leaving him, too. I made sure not to make eye contact with him as I gathered my things, acting as if it was no big deal. I believe that the calmer you are as a dog owner, the more chilled out your dog will be. Not so with Jasper as a puppy.

I gathered him next to his crate and got some biscuits out, I kissed his head, and while outwardly I looked fine, I was churning inside. And he knew it. I had to push his rear end into the crate.

I shut the crate door and latched it. It was like the sound of a cell block gate on death row. Then I pushed a couple of treats through the gaps.

I kept it together and said, in my best authoritative Mary Poppins imitation, "Have a nap, and I'll be back soon." (Yes, to me, Mary Poppins sounds authoritative. I follow the rules!)

My eyes betrayed me. I was as worried and upset as he was.

I walked out of our front door and started down the long hall to the elevators. I got about ten paces when I heard something I'd never heard before. It was a pathetic wail mixed with a moan and a yelp (which is not all that unusual in New York City, but still…).

Was that…Jasper?

I slowed but then thought, "I'll let him cry it out," and kept walking. But I lived in an apartment with a ton of neighbors, and the cries were getting louder with every step. I'd never heard anything like that. It certainly would have been considered a violation under the Geneva Convention.

And so, against everything I knew to do when training a dog, I ran back to the apartment. I tried to calm him through the crate, but he wouldn't settle. I begged him to cooperate. "I've gotta go to work, Jasper. Please." He was inconsolable.

So I let him out of the crate and picked him up, and he whimpered as he nuzzled his nose under my chin.

I texted the dog sitter with one hand as I held Jasper in the other. She said she was just fifteen minutes away, but that's what she'd said fifteen minutes ago. I either had to try again or I'd have to take him with me to the studio.

I decided to try again. I put him back in his crate, said with a firm voice that he would be fine, and left, a bit tearful. As soon as the door shut, he wailed louder than before.

So, what did I do? The wrong thing.

I opened the door and went back in. I knew right then that I'd made a rod for my own back.

I took him out of the crate and sat with my back against the wall and my legs crossed. He climbed into that circle and pressed against me while

I calmed him down. I told him I wouldn't leave him alone, and he didn't have to worry.

The dog sitter arrived a few minutes later and I rushed to the studio, breaking a sweat by the time I jogged over to Times Square from Hell's Kitchen. I had the dreadful feeling of being a bad dog parent.

In that instant when I turned back, Jasper and I established a pattern that is still very hard to break.

After that incident, I felt that I couldn't leave Jasper alone. When Peter was away and I had to work or we had a dinner to go to, I hired Kyra, the sitter that used to look after Henry in his final days, to take care of Jasper. Kyra was a pre-med student and would come to our apartment and study, walk and feed Jasper, and have him all tired out by the time I got home. We still rely on her. She's been a great help, and I never worry when Kyra's there.

When we moved to the new apartment to be closer to Central Park, Jasper was older and I thought he could handle being alone. But one night when I was a last-minute fill-in host for Greta Van Susteren, who wasn't feeling well, I found out I was wrong. I'd asked the dog walker to keep him until after I got home at 11 p.m., but it was a Friday night and she had plans. She said she could drop him off at 9:30 p.m., and that was the best we could do under the circumstances. I thought it would be fine because he'd be so tired after being out all day.

When I finished the broadcast, I turned on my phone during the ride home. I had seven messages from the new building's management. Our new apartment was in a very established building of condominiums—it was as sophisticated a place as I'd ever lived, and I was making a terrible first impression.

Jasper had been wailing after the dog walker had dropped him off, and my neighbors were both alarmed and concerned. I knew precisely what Jasper could sound like when he was really laying it on thick—it was the sound he made that got me to come back that first time. Dogs learn fast. Too bad I didn't.

I came home and held a trembling Jasper for an hour on the couch. We sat in silence as I soothed him and calmed myself. I'd screwed up everything for the both of us by making him so afraid to be alone and indulging his puppy cries. I didn't leave his sight that entire weekend.

What was I going to do now?

This is a bit embarrassing to admit, but I started making up reasons why I couldn't go somewhere outside of work. I handle the social calendar for Peter and me, and I politely turned down dinner and party invitations so that we didn't have to leave Jasper alone. I thought Peter didn't know what I was doing, but he was on to me. He just shook his head and said, "You love him. I get it."

When we did have to leave Jasper alone, I would get knots in my stomach that started several hours before the separation. I never canceled on an event just because of this problem, but it crossed my mind.

This is what separation anxiety looks like.

I came up with weird ways to manage it. Since I didn't want to be the last one Jasper saw when we were leaving, I'd ask Peter if it was okay that I left first. That way it didn't look to Jasper as if I was abandoning him.

If I was the last one to leave him, Jasper would cry. When Peter did it, Jasper was fine. Jasper knew who the soft touch was, and he played me like a lute. (Well, maybe not a lute. Who really plays a lute?) So I made Peter be the bad guy.

I'd get my coat and say, "Your daddy is here, Jasper." Then I'd sneak out the door, making sure it made little noise when it shut, and head down to the lobby. Peter would wait a couple of minutes, then get his coat. He'd settle Jasper in his dog bed and give him a treat before joining me downstairs to hail a taxi.

"Is he okay?" I'd ask.

"Of course he's okay, my darling. Don't worry," Peter said. He never said he thought I was crazy. He didn't have to.

When we'd get to the restaurant, friends would ask us how Jasper was doing. I'd say that he was great except that he had terrible separation anxiety.

"It isn't Jasper," Peter said, slyly pointing a finger in my direction.

The nice thing is that Peter didn't hold my anxiety against me or get irritated, though he would have been justified. Peter saw the love I felt, knew that I couldn't rationalize my emotions, and he adjusted so that I could be the kind of dog mom I wanted to be.

"And you make fun of helicopter parents on *The Five*?" he joked.

Eventually, we got to a point where we can leave Jasper in the apartment (no crate) and there's no wailing. And I no longer get teary about him being on his own. Though I still sometimes hire Kyra—I call her Jasper's girlfriend so that he doesn't think he needs a babysitter.

But I'm not crazy . . . right?

Dog Park Rules

IN THE LAST EIGHTEEN YEARS, one of my favorite places to go is the dog park. When I was growing up, there was no such thing, but dog ownership has changed and now in cities all across America you can find off-leash dog parks. This is a good thing. You see all kinds of dogs (and people!) at the dog park, from the breed standards to the rescue animals, and no matter where I go, the dog park always makes me happy.

My first dog park was in Lytham-St. Anne's in the UK. I started going there when Henry was a puppy and had received all of his shots. The park ran along the beach in the sand dunes, and we nicknamed it "The Dog Poop Park." It wasn't an official dog park, but all the dog owners gathered there in the mornings and late afternoons. No one hassled us.

At the beach, we'd walk along the dunes and the dogs would run around us. I used to pray that the Whippet would be there because it would run so fast and tire Henry out.

During the summer, we'd stay out there for hours because it was light until 11 p.m. Then, in the winter, the sun rose around 9 a.m. and went down around 3:30 p.m. It was quite a contrast (and I lasted only one winter!).

I made friends with a woman that had a year-old Great Dane, and Henry and Boo-Boo (short for Bublich) became great pals. Henry used to clamp onto Boo-Boo's jowls and hold on while he loped along. Sometimes after the morning walks, Henry and I would go over to their house and sit in front of the fire. I would drink tea while Henry would get so close to the fire and sleep so soundly, I was afraid he would cook.

In San Diego, we had one of the best dog parks—Del Mar dog beach. What joy!

Henry learned to surf the waves, we walked barefoot in the sand, and we watched the sun set over the ocean all year round. Later we moved closer to downtown, and on the weekends we'd go over to Coronado Island where there's a dog beach just south of the navy base. Henry would swim so far out he'd surprise some of the surfers—"Hey, look at that dog!"

We'd watch dogs run around together, and some were sneaky enough to put their snouts into the coolers next to the beach towels and pull out any food they could find. Others would "mark" someone's chair while the humans weren't looking. It was great fun.

After we moved closer to downtown, we started taking Henry to Grape Street Dog Park, which was designated as a leash-free area. But as dog owners know, our rights to have places where we can run our dogs around without a leash are constantly under threat.

Nothing can unite a group of dog owners more than the worry that their dog park will be closed down. And

that's what happened at Grape Street.

A couple of neighbors had complained to the city council about the dog park, and a local council member proposed a large reduction in the area for dogs, and she also proposed fencing them in.

Naturally, we were a bit upset about it. I had never before been part of an organized protest, but I was prepared to go boneless and to jail if that's what it was going to take to keep the park open.

A hearing was set by which both sides' arguments would be heard, and of those who attended, the support in favor of maintaining the park status quo was something on the order of 100 to 2.

Jasper as a puppy,
in Central Park in the fall.

At the hearing, one of the dissenters complained that the dogs urinated in the park—and a supporter pointed out that dogs urinate whether they're on or off the leash.

Peter made the point that more than a third of U.S. households have dogs.

"Here in the United States, particularly in California, just about any minority that protests gets equal rights. But dog owners continue to be treated as second-class citizens," he said, as only someone with a British accent can.

The council member, seeing that she was outnumbered and that her constituents were clearly against the idea, changed her position at the meeting.

Grape Street Dog Park was saved! And that's how government by the people (and their dogs) should work!

When we moved to Washington, D.C., we rented a small row house on Capitol Hill and our morning walks with Henry were in Lincoln Park—an unofficial dog park where most people didn't mind. I say *most* (see Peter's story about his encounter with Officer Smith of the Park Police).

This was the most bipartisan dog run in Washington. No one cared who anyone worked for, and in fact, some alliances were made as people from different sides of the aisle figured out how to advance legislation or policy by teaming up. The dogs brought us together.

There's also the Congressional Cemetery in Southeast D.C. that we could walk to. For years the cemetery was neglected and it fell into disrepair and was an area for drug dealers. Christ Church and the K-9 Corps got together and helped clean up the area and drove away the drug dealers.

From then on, people on Capitol Hill could become members of the historical society and pay to have the privilege of walking their dogs without leashes on the grounds. I was very uncomfortable at first—it seemed wrong to have dogs running around the gravesites. But one day, a regular visitor told me that I needed to get over it—she said that she believed the people buried there would have been glad to know that the dogs could have fun right there in the city.

I decided to take her advice and it became one of my favorite places to walk in D.C.

It was kind of funny when we'd ask Henry, "Do you want to go to the cemetery?" in a Scooby-Doo voice. Cemeteries never sounded so fun! And as Peter says, "People are dying to get in there."

On weekends we'd drive up to Annapolis and visit a park that had a dog beach. It was a tiny beach and there weren't any waves, but it was a great escape from Washington and a place where I could sit and look at the water and not at my e-mails.

When we turned into the park, Henry would be up and have his head out the window. We'd taught him to bark once for please and twice for thank you—which was charming and of course gave us some bragging rights as owners of a clever and polite dog—but Henry loved swimming so much that he would just start barking

Henry in D.C.'s Congressional Cemetery—where the neighborhood dog owners joined the Historical Society to support the upkeep and to walk our dogs. Jasper stops there on his travels back and forth to South Carolina.

as loud as he could, sometimes right in our ears. "Please! Please! Please!"

Down at the beach, we'd try to get Henry, who was quite athletic, to jump off the dock into the water. He would not. Then one day, a collie came running down the dock and jumped off to get the toy his owner had thrown in the water. Everyone clapped and cheered. And you can imagine what happened next.

Henry was like, "I can do that, too." But his version was more of a belly flop than a leap. It was adorable,

Henry in Annapolis. Look at that happy face!

though it seemed like it would hurt, especially when he did it over and over for an hour.

Years later we made sure to teach Jasper to leap in, and some of his best photos are at our friends' pools—Henry would be a little proud and a lot jealous.

• • •

Never in my life would I have imagined that the best American dog park is in the middle of America's most populated city—Manhattan. But Central Park is leash-free from 6 a.m. to 9 a.m., and it is one of the best things about New York City.

Peter and Jasper go every morning from 7:30 to 9 a.m., and I join them when I can.

The dogs are surprisingly well behaved, and for the most part the owners are very attentive and watch their dogs carefully. The commuters take it in stride, and everything goes pretty smoothly.

It is wonderful in all seasons—even in winter. The ice skating rink opens early, so on our walks we stop to watch the young students twirl around with the Central Park South skyline behind them.

There's a gentle man who appears to be homeless on the other side of that pond who brings bread to feed the ducks and other birds, and he and Jasper have become friends. Jasper stops every day and the man gives him a bit of bread. "Just two, please. Thank you so much." And he never gives Jasper more than two, even though I can tell he wants to. Jasper makes him smile, and the man makes us more mindful and compassionate.

Some days we put Jasper on his leash to walk through the Central Park Zoo, then we go back up to the Mall,

lined with mature American elms, where he makes a beeline for the Bethesda Fountain.

Recently when Peter's grandkids were visiting we watched *Home Alone 2: Lost in New York*, and when a scene with that fountain came up they exclaimed, "That's Jasper's fountain!"

Once we make that loop, we're back by the baseball fields and the rest of the gang has gathered.

Jasper is one of the fastest at the park (naturally!), and his game of tug-of-war is admirable.

The dogs all recognize Peter—he's the Pied Piper with the best treats. He knows all of their names and how many treats they're allowed to have. It's such a joy to watch. And like kids at the swimming pool, the dogs all start playing again as soon as you make a move to head home.

We're often late getting back, but we don't mind. Central Park with the dogs is the very best way to begin every morning.

Jasper watching the ice skaters in Central Park.

DANA'S RULES FOR A GREAT DOG PARK EXPERIENCE:

Rules for dogs:

- ✓ No sitting. If you lie down, we're going home. You have to keep moving.
- ✓ No fighting—dog fights will ruin the experience for everyone and force the city government to get involved. So none of that.
- ✓ No jumping—especially on commuters! Ruining someone's new suit is a sure way to get us all in trouble.
- ✓ No begging. It is so unbecoming.

Rules for humans:

- ✓ No politics—why ruin a perfectly good morning walk with the dogs by talking about politics.
- ✓ No work complaints—keep the park a special place, limit the negativity.
- ✓ No worries—set aside the day for a bit, enjoy the dogs. Try to leave your phone at home or in your pocket. Your life will improve.

All over the world, dog parks are the same. The people come to exercise their dogs, to get fresh air, and to be a little social. No one dresses up to go to the dog park. Hardly anyone knows each other's names, certainly not their last names.

I recently asked Peter, "What does Stefan do for a living?"

"I have no idea. I never thought to ask him," he said. Good answer!

We have been going for enough years now that we know a lot of the owners. We have had to say good-bye to some folks who've moved away, and comforted a couple of owners whose dogs have died. We've welcomed new puppies and new babies. It's like an extended family that only ever meets outdoors.

About two years after we'd moved to New York City, I was struggling to enjoy the city itself. I was nervous as a cat in the traffic, and I hated all of the noise—not just from the cars, trucks, and buses, but from the yelling and the couple that plays the bongos outside my window, and all the guys that have saxophones and can barely play a tune.

The weather was getting to me— too hot or too cold. I missed seeing the sky. I was in a rotten mood about New York, and I was thinking about leaving. But I loved my job on *The Five* at Fox News, and I couldn't do that job anywhere else. I needed an attitude adjustment.

On New Year's Eve, I made a resolution to write down one thing a day I liked about New York. At first it was hard to come up with an answer. I would write them down on my Jasper calendar, and after several weeks, this exercise started to help me change my opinion about the city.

When I flip back through it now, I realize that 80 percent of the time I had the same answer, "Central Park dog park."

The park—its beauty and the friends we've made there (including the dog friends)—has been the best thing about living in New York City. I feel most like my real self when I'm at the dog park in the middle of Manhattan.

And that's quite a statement coming from a girl who started out on a ranch in Wyoming! 🐾

The Protest Pee

Jasper trained us well. His separation anxiety became ours, or at least mine, and we adjusted our lives to deal with it.

Peter and I would stagger our workouts and evenings out in a way that made sure Jasper wasn't ever on his own. It was the wrong way to handle the problem, but it actually made things easier. And it meant that I didn't have to worry, either. Who really had the anxiety? Wait. Don't answer that.

One night, for fun and out of desperation, I asked my Twitter and Facebook followers for suggestions on dealing with a pet's separation anxiety. I got tons of advice.

I tried a few of the suggestions, such as putting him in a ThunderShirt, which is not a heavy metal band but rather a tight-fitting garment used for dogs afraid of thunderstorms. Dogs are supposed to feel more secure in a snug shirt. That didn't work for Jasper, but he looked pretty cute in it.

Most of the suggestions involved crating him whenever we left the apartment. But it was too late for that. Just you try to get Jasper to go in a crate as a grown dog. He's more stubborn than a mule. It's not happening.

Suitcases were the worst. If we had to travel and brought out a suitcase, Jasper would mope and was, as Peter said, "all boot-faced." I tried getting him to ignore the suitcase by making a fuss of him or giving him a toy or a treat. I was not rewarded with even a wag of his tail. I tried not looking at him at all and just packing as if it was situation normal. I'd also try reasoning with him. "It's only two days," I said. But two days and two minutes is the same to Jasper. He has no sense of how long we're gone— just that we're away.

Only one thing works when we're packing. If Jasper is going on a trip with us, we set out his bag, a fancy red, white, and blue tote made from sailcloth in Annapolis, by the front door. He learned that meant he's going, too, and that perks him right up.

Of course, then he follows us from room to room as we get ready, and dashes out the door before we do so that he's not left behind. As if he's some sort of furry Macaulay Culkin (actually, Mr. Culkin is looking a little furry himself these days…). I've been tempted to put his bag out even if he's not going with us, but I can't lie, even to my dog.

We also found ourselves accepting any invitation to visit friends, especially outside of the city, if Jasper could come along, too. We are blessed to know a lot of people who love dogs, and some whose kids want a dog but they're not able to have one, and so we became frequent if perhaps shameless weekend houseguests all around the area. You don't have to ask me twice.

When I wrote *And the Good News Is . . .* I received a lot of gifts for Jasper, including an embroidered quilt with the Great Seal of the United States. It is beautiful and functional. We take it with us to our friends' homes if we are invited to stay the night, because, well, you try telling Jasper he can't sleep on the bed. With the quilt, we're covered. Literally and figuratively.

When we're at our place in South Carolina, leaving him in the house is even more stressful. For a while, whenever we'd go out, we'd come home and find that he'd peed on the floor. As soon as we'd walk in, we'd know something happened, because Jasper would grab a toy as he always does, but instead of frantic joy and butt wagging, his tail would be down and he'd look guilty. It was hard to discipline him because you're supposed to catch them in the act. Peter would get pretty mad at Jasper, and I'd feel terrible.

"He's so scared to be left alone," I'd say.

"No, he's being a brat," Peter responded.

We compromised and called it a protest pee (maybe he learned it from

Occupy Wall Street). He knew what he was doing was wrong, but he couldn't help himself. At one point I found a wet spot on a new light blue rattan rug. I was mad and I told him to "Come here. Now."

I didn't know Peter was filming the scene on his phone, but he caught everything. Jasper wouldn't run away from me, but he wouldn't come either. I tried pulling him by the collar, but he wouldn't budge. I tried pulling him by his front legs, but he dug his back paws into the ground and wouldn't move. I got behind him and was finally able to drag him over to the spot where I scolded him. I really let him have it. And then I felt awful. At least he never peed on that rug again!

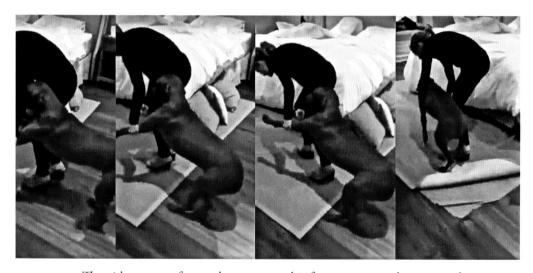

The video was so funny that we posted it for everyone to have a good laugh at my expense.

I laughed, too. Eventually.

You're Back! Here's a Stuffed Animal Carcass

BRACE YOURSELF! should be a warning sign on our front door.

Jasper loves to greet people. Whenever someone comes in, he checks out who it is, then scrambles to his toy box and brings something back, his behind wagging so much it could churn butter.

We taught him not to jump up on people, so instead he does these little hops on his front legs. He looks like Peter dancing to hip-hop.

He doesn't want you to take the toy from him; he just wants you to see it. And if we tell him, "Get another one," he'll return to the box and stuff another toy or two in his mouth. We praise him, his tail wags even more. His record was five toys at once—quite a mouthful.

Like other dogs, Jasper doesn't have a keen sense of time. We get this kind of greeting if we've been away for a week, popped out to the grocery store, or taken out the trash.

Jasper greets me with more than one toy in his mouth. His record is five (of course).

No matter what, Jasper greets us like we're just back from the front. (Which, working in cable news in New York City, I often feel that I am.)

Being greeted by Jasper, and Henry before him, is a rush for me. Like a runner's high without the workout. It means I'm always met with warmth and affection—and it helps make our house such a welcoming home.

From the start, Jasper loved his toys and his bed. It looked like he would make up games to play by himself, and he'd make all kinds of groaning and howling noises, just for the fun of it. To this day when we make him go to his bed while we eat dinner, he will put on one of these displays—turning upside down, and having some sort of play fight with a ghost, something he's done since his first days in Manhattan. It never fails to crack us up—which is probably why he does it. Those moments take the sting out of any work day.

Jasper has a gigantic basket of toys. Many of them now are just carcasses of stuffed animals. Toys I can see from where I'm writing: snake, lobster, dinosaur, elephant, circus elephant, duck, bear, killer whale, sock monkey (a favorite), Frisbee, red panda, and a hippie man. Hippie man is dressed in a tie-dye T-shirt and has a long beard and a peace symbol necklace. Jasper ripped off his arms. Peter says, "Don't worry, Jasper. He's armless." I laugh every time.

One of the reasons Jasper rips apart his toys is that he's trying to get the squeak out. I've watched him with new toys and admire how he can immediately find the weak stitching and start pulling it apart. Once he gets the plastic squeaker out of the toy, he ejects it onto the floor. Another one bites the dust.

We have a friend that patches up all of his dog's ripped-up toys, painstakingly sewing them on weekends. That would never work at our house. If I tried to sew Jasper's toys, I wouldn't have time for anything else. I'm just glad he doesn't do that to the couch. Or one of our guests.

Every few weeks I think that I need to pare down his toys. I wait until he's out with Peter and then I start going through the box. Every toy brings back a memory. I remember if the toy was a gift, like his Tigger that my sister, Angie, got him when he was just a young puppy. I can't throw that out. I pick up others, some now just the hides of old skunks and squirrels, and still I can't throw them away. I could end up on *Hoarders* but instead of having tons of live pets, I would be surrounded by the remnants of Jasper's toys. Needless to say, despite my determination to declutter the toy box, I don't throw much away. Essentially, we live in a stuffed pet cemetery.

Jasper & friends. Peter helps me stage these— though he grumbles, I think he gets a kick out of it.

"OUCH!" is often yelled in our house when we step on one of Jasper's deer antler chew toys that he's left lying in the middle of the rug. Jasper's toys aren't just in the box. They're in the kitchen, the family room, the hallway, the living room, the bedroom…even in the bathroom. They're everywhere. We're forever picking up his toys and putting them back in the box.

But sometimes, Peter and I just walk over them. One week an "indestructible" stuffed pink pig sat in our hallway for days. I refused to pick it up, and I wanted to test Peter on how long it would stay there.

On the third day, I was getting irritated. "Peter, are you ever going to pick up that pig?" I asked.

"I hadn't noticed it," he said. I didn't believe him at first, but then I realized I ignore the toys, too. It isn't that unusual to take a bath and have a stuffed cow and a scraggly monkey sitting on the floor staring at me (which sounds like a scene from a Hitchcock movie, I'll admit).

On a night when Peter and Jasper were both away, I came home late from the studio and turned on the bedroom light. I yelped because I thought there was a raccoon in the bedroom (fifteen floors up in Manhattan, mind you)—but it was just one of Jasper's toys, placed just so. Very funny, Jasper.

Jasper's toys have kind of become our friends, too. We're a growing family. I just wish I'd taught him to put the toys back in the box. But even Henry couldn't do that.

One of my favorite photographs to stage is Jasper with all of his "friends" getting ready to watch a presidential debate. When he was just a young puppy, I made Peter help me gather all of the toys and pile them up around Jasper on the couch. Peter thought it was a bit ridiculous and over the top, but he rallied and that particular photograph ended up being one of my most popular on Twitter. Since the number of toys keeps growing, the number of "friends" does, too—but many of them are looking a little worse for wear since their stuffing has been ripped out.

Jasper and all of his friends getting ready to watch the presidential debate in 2012. That was one of my most popular Tweets—and still one of my favorites.

Just another night on the couch with Jasper and his buddies—talk about a popular dog.

My favorite thing to do when I get home from work on some days is to go into one of Jasper's dedicated cupboards in the kitchen (yes, there is more than one!) and pull out a new toy. He must know the smell because he comes trotting in as I say, "Oh my goodness…oh my goodness! What is this? It's a (fill in the blank)." You could give him anything and he'd be so thrilled. I once gave him a stuffed Larry King doll. He even loved that.

Peter used to prove this to me when Henry was alive. He'd say, of course he wags his tail when you talk in that voice. Then he'd demonstrate. "Henry! Do you want to go to the electric chair? Oh you do! You want to go to the electric chair!"

Tail wagged. Point taken.

But I'm still not throwing any of those toys out.

Dana's Personal Tips for Dog Training

I'M NOT A PROFESSIONAL DOG TRAINER, but I grew up on a ranch that had both working and house dogs that were well behaved and a lot of fun. They were a part of our family.

At night, after supper, they got our scraps. They even liked watermelon rinds and sometimes would fight over them. I never liked to give the dogs the bucket of scraps because they scared me with their enthusiasm and sometimes they'd snap at each other, showing their teeth and growling. So I watched my cousins do it. They were not afraid.

When I trained my own dogs years later, I tried to incorporate my grandfather's techniques (even though Jasper lives in Manhattan and not on a ranch, these tips are universal).

Many families choose to hire a professional dog trainer, and that's a good option if you don't have the time to train your dog yourself. But if you want to try to do it on your own, there are several good books and online videos that can help you. And in the meantime, here are some of my top tips for dog training:

➤ **START EARLY.** Dogs like to learn, and the best way to train is to start as early as possible. This goes for everything from potty training to tricks. If you've opened your heart and home to a rescue and aren't sure of its age, consider asking a professional to help you. Often, rescue dogs know they've been saved, and so they express their gratitude by being good and sweet.

➤ **CONSISTENCY.** This is so important—everyone in the household has to agree on the approach to training the dog. Each person must use the same commands and no one can be the pushover and let the dog get away with something that others wouldn't allow. Establish someone to be in charge for particular outings or training sessions—that way the dog doesn't have multiple people yelling different things at it all at once (you can rotate the person in charge so that the dog learns to respond to everyone in the family).

> **EYE CONTACT**. When you're interacting with your dog, always try to look him in the eye. You'll notice that when a dog knows he has done something wrong, he looks away and avoids your gaze. So make sure that you look the dog in his eyes and say the words for the behavior you're trying to enforce (this is important for whether you're disciplining or praising your dog). Also, let him know he is loved and safe. At least once a day I make sure to look Jasper in the eyes and say, "I love you." I think he understands me.

Eye contact is key.

> **MANNERS MATTER**. Since we live in a highly populated area and share elevators with people in our building, we've put a focus on manners. Jasper knows he has to sit in an elevator and that he can't pull on a leash when we are on sidewalks. Thankfully, the only time he barks is when he's playing at the dog park. We discouraged him from barking inside from an early age so that we wouldn't bother our neighbors. I also refuse to embarrass myself by having to yell at my dog in public, and so I make sure my dogs know how to behave. Gradually, after they learn to heel or sit at the corner before crossing a street, I don't even give them a command—I just clear my throat, "Ahem . . . ," and they do what I want. This saves me from being

exasperated out in public and it's made all of our outings better—taking your dog out should be a joy, not a chore.

➤ **PRACTICE MAKES PERFECT**. Repetition is the key to good dog training. If you're trying to get your dog to heel or to give a high five, it's important to practice regularly and often. I've found that practicing three times a day is the minimum needed for a dog to learn. Some dogs catch on quickly, especially if every time they give a high five they think they're going to receive a treat. I've also found that you have to give dogs a break—after five times, if the dog has the trick down, move on and then try it again a couple of hours later. If the dog doesn't seem to be getting it after five tries, give it a rest for a while. You can revisit that trick later.

➤ **CALM OWNER, CALMER DOG**. A hyper or frantic dog can make for an unhappy household. Vizslas are known to have a lot of energy, and I've noticed that if we are calm around Jasper, then he's calm. We make sure he gets enough time to exercise and play, but we don't put up with whining or obnoxious behavior. Dogs will mimic your demeanor, so a calm owner helps train a calmer dog.

➤ **HIDE FROM YOUR DOG ONCE WHEN THEY'RE YOUNG AND THEY'LL ALWAYS KEEP YOU IN SIGHT**. This was a tip we learned in England when we had just picked up Henry from the breeder. We read that if you wanted to make sure your dog wouldn't run off, the best way to do that was to hide from them, giving them a scare. We tried this at a forested rest area. Henry was off his leash but safe in an enclosed space. He started sniffing around and when he wasn't looking, Peter dashed behind a tree and waited, keeping an eye on our new puppy. Henry didn't notice for a while, but when he looked up and couldn't see his owner, he panicked and started dashing about. We let it go on for a few seconds, and then Peter stepped out from behind the tree. Henry ran to him and we soothed him, letting him know he was okay. But guess what? From then on we could go for a hike or a walk on the beach and he never got too far away from us. Those few moments of fear were worth it. We didn't have to yell constantly at Henry while we were walking, and that made for more enjoyment for the rest of us. We did the same with Jasper and got the identical result.

➤ **PATIENCE**. As much as it seems like they can understand you, they can't always know what you want. Give them a pass if they can't figure it out right away. I taught Henry the names of his toys when he was a small puppy, and he could pull out all the ones I would ask for. Jasper, on the other hand, didn't pick that up as easily and I had to realize he wasn't going to be just like Henry. Being more patient with Jasper helped both of us relax.

➤ **EASY ON THE TREATS**. Find some low-calorie treats and cut them in half or thirds. And don't always give food to reinforce good behavior. Dogs want to please their owners, so make a fuss of them—that's as good as a treat for most dogs. Keeping a dog fit is the owner's responsibility—take it seriously. Preventing a dog from getting overweight is important for their health, especially their hearts. And my motto is "a fit dog is a fun dog."

➤ **LET DOGS PLAY**. Dogs need exercise and they love to have fun. Make time to take them to play with other dogs, and when they bring you a rope to pull or a ball to throw, put down your phone and give them a few minutes. I remember that Henry hated my BlackBerry—he would sulk when I would tap out e-mails when I was supposed to be walking with him. He made me pay more attention to him. Now, when I go to the dog park, I allow myself only two e-mail checks (and that's when I usually post a photo of Jasper—rules are made to be broken if a cute picture is involved). So let your dogs play and have fun—and you'll end up enjoying yourself more, too. 🐾

Dogus Interruptus

I've come to appreciate the differences between Henry's and Jasper's personalities, but there are some traditions I carried into Jasper's life after Henry died. For example, I tell Jasper that we have to put on his necklace to go outside. It's just a regular collar, but it sounds more special if I call it a necklace. Which is kind of like calling ground chuck "Salisbury steak."

I also came up with a kiss attack game that both of our dogs loved. Peter and I will slowly come at Jasper from either side and I'll whisper, "We're gonna get you…We're gonna get you…" and Jasper sits there in anticipation, not moving anything but his eyes, and when we get close enough I give the signal and then we give him a kiss attack, smooching him as fast and as many times as we can.

One thing we vowed not to do with Jasper is to give him as many table scraps as we gave Henry. I used to feed Henry half of my plate, and I snuck food to Henry when I thought Peter wasn't looking, then Peter wouldn't give me a hard time about not eating enough. Of course, Peter says he always knew when I'd given my dinner to Henry because (a) he wasn't blind and (b) I was snappy when I hadn't eaten enough. True on both counts.

I've long wondered if giving Henry so many table scraps affected his health later on. I know that most dogs live only to thirteen or fourteen, so Henry had a long life for a dog. But I believe he would have been healthier and maybe not have contracted Cushing's disease with a more healthful diet.

Jasper gets a mix of kibble and grain-free protein, and on weekends I'll make him some scrambled or poached eggs if we're having the same. He loves bully sticks, which are a good chewy treat, but they smell disgusting.

Once at a friend's house, they'd bought Jasper a Texas Taffy bully stick to chew while we watched a football game. The husband of the couple almost threw up. He is an NYPD detective and he said that while he'd smelled plenty of dead bodies, bully sticks were much worse. It smelled awful to me, too, but I laughed so hard I cried.

Meanwhile, Jasper was unaware of the problem his treat was causing. He just chomped on it and ignored our cries to open the windows. Too bad they got the extra-large size.

And there's a new treat he's been getting. I hate to admit it, but how can I resist? At our favorite restaurant in South Carolina we take our friends and sit outside with our dogs, and I splurge on a side of bacon. But it isn't for me. The dogs get to share it. They love it and I get a kick out of watching them devour it.

A special treat that only I give to Jasper is a spot of lotion on his paws. Most dogs love lotion, especially after you've just come out of the shower and moisturized. It's cute, but no one wants their dog to lick off their lotion.

So instead of yelling at him, I taught Jasper to lie down and stick out his paws. Then I put a little dab on the top of each paw and he gets to lick it off.

"You want your lotion?" I ask him at night when he comes in before bed. He gets so excited and Peter just shakes his head, bemused, as Jasper and I do our thing. When Jasper goes to stay the night at someone's house while we're traveling, I note this little tradition in case they want to try it, too.

As an adult, I swore our dogs would never sleep all night in bed with us. For years, I've fallen asleep on Peter's shoulder and that's still my favorite spot—where I feel closest to him and safest in the world. Unfortunately, Peter has to travel a lot, and when Jasper and I were alone, I lost all of my "no dogs in the bed" willpower one night.

The entire time Jasper had lived with us, he'd slept on his little bed next to Peter, boxed in with suitcases and cardboard boxes so he couldn't wander around in the night. Peter would drape his hand over the bed and settle Jasper down if he woke up, and we'd look at each other and giggle when Jasper would yawn in the morning—you've never heard such a high-pitched squeal. Then we'd try to sneak pictures of Jasper as he learned how to clean his face and lay on his back playing with a toy. It was a small bedroom, a tight squeeze with our bed, nightstands, dresser, and puppy. But there was no place else I'd rather be.

So, back to my weak moment that changed everything. Peter was away and I had been late at work one night. A sitter had taken care of Jasper and when I got home, it was time for bed. I got ready and put Jasper into his bed and made sure the suitcases were in place to block his way.

I turned out the light and said good night. There's enough ambient light in New York City that the room wasn't completely dark, and I could see that Jasper wasn't settling down. He was just sitting on the floor, his head now tall enough to see over the mattress. He was staring at me.

"Go to bed, Jasper," I said.

He didn't move. He just stared. If a dog can look incredulous, he did.

"Now, Jasper. Go to bed!" I raised my voice. Still he didn't move. I turned over so that I couldn't see him, hoping that he'd realize it was time to go to sleep. But he didn't move. He was playing the game of statue with me, and he was winning.

Feeling his eyes on me, I said again, "Jasper, go to bed now!"

Then I decided to ignore him. If he didn't want to sleep but instead chose to sit there looking at me, I'd leave him to it.

But he kept staring. I could feel his eyes on me. And I was feeling lonely and restless, too.

"Well, maybe if he just sleeps with me when Peter is gone…No, that's a terrible idea," I thought.

And then, in a moment of exasperation and weakness, without turning around to face him, I reached my hand back and patted the bed. Jasper recognized the invitation, and he was up like a shot, curling into the backs of my legs. It was so cozy.

"Oh, Jasper. We are in so much trouble," I said. But I smiled and fell asleep.

I'd broken the seal. And he's shared our bed ever since.

I try to make room for him while also sleeping on Peter's shoulder, but sometimes that's uncomfortable. I've tried putting him on the other side of us, so that I'm in the middle, but that doesn't work because Jasper likes to be in the middle.

Jasper and his sock monkey, sleeping on the bed.

"Dogus interruptus," Peter calls Jasper.

So then we tell him to go to his own bed and he does...for a while. Sometimes in the middle of the night, I'll hear Jasper get up and walk over to my side of the bed (not Peter's—he knows who will cave), and he shakes his ears and sits down and stares at me. I wait a bit, and then I just pat the bed. Up he comes. He still likes to spoon into me, but I have to brace myself—Jasper curls around, gearing up, and then slams into me. We laugh and then Peter and I hold hands on top of Jasper's flank. No wonder he likes to be in the bed with us. It's a family cuddle.

And it all started with a moment of weakness on my part. Now it's a strength. Why? Because Jasper has helped me relax and not be so uptight. I don't have to rigidly follow the rules anymore. And that's made life a lot more fun.

Jasper is such a good companion. He'll do whatever we're doing—follow a soccer match on TV, cheer for a team, settle down for a nap. He spends a lot of time standing on his two back legs using a counter for support. And he and never sits on the floor—he prefers to sit on the furniture. My friend Jeanie Mamo has always thought Jasper thinks he's human.

Getting up on the furniture was a big no-no for dogs in my house growing up (the cats had no such rule). And Henry didn't particularly like to get up on the couch, unless he was told he could and even then he'd last only a while because he got too hot sitting next to us.

My lap dog. Greg Gutfeld took this picture to try to show people how small I am.

Jasper, on the other hand, never saw a chair or sofa he didn't think he had the right to get up on. He sits up and stares straight ahead, sometimes watching TV, acting like a person. His favorite show, of course, is *Wheel of Fortune*. Followed by *The Five* and football.

He particularly likes it if there's a person already sitting in the chair. He clambers up and will always find—or make—room to sit next to whoever is sitting, no matter how small the chair is. And this is not a small dog.

On my rocking chair in the bedroom where I write, he will sit at my feet and look at me, ignoring my suggestion that he choose the bed so that I can study for the show. Eventually, because it is hard to work when someone is staring at you (unless you're an actor), I invite him up.

Jasper weighs about sixty-four pounds and is tall and lean. That makes getting up and turning around a bit of a challenge. But he's never failed to curl up and squeeze in right beside me. He sits straight up for a long time, resisting sleep. When his head and his eyes get too heavy, he'll give in and negotiate for some more room on the chair. That gives him nowhere to rest his head except for on my arm or my keyboard. And still, I adjust. I use his back as a table to rest my computer, or I type at an angle with my head cocked to one side so that I can see the screen straight on. It gives me a real pain in the neck.

Peter gets the same treatment. Jasper lies next to him all day while Peter works from the sofa. Sometimes when Peter has had conference calls, he's had to apologize for Jasper barking—he also wants international clients to know it's not *him* making strange noises. A few times Jasper has ended up in the screen shot during a Skype call and thankfully, the clients on the other end laughed. They either thought it was charming or that Jasper was the sales rep. It really is a one-man-and-his-dog operation.

At night when we're cleaning up the dishes or getting ready for bed, Peter or I will make excuses for staying put, saying, "I'd get up, honey, but…the dog." And because we don't want to disturb him, neither of us minds doing the dishes. (I just try to be the one that happens to be trapped by the dog.)

It's a dog's life in our house. Happily so.

Nonstop Jasper Chatter

Dog people will totally understand what I mean about the nonstop conversation about the family dog. Even if you plan a romantic date night, it's inevitable that a couple will start talking about their dog. It's the safe, happy topic that everyone goes to when they've caught up with each other on work and hobbies and news from the family that wasn't already posted on Facebook.

Peter and I do this with Jasper all the time.

"What's he like?" It's a British saying that I picked up when we lived together in England. It's a generic question that leads into a list of some of Jasper's attributes and stories about him that we haven't yet shared with each other. "You should have seen him at the bank today…" Peter will say, delighting me with a story that would bore anyone else to tears.

When that part of the conversation dries up, I'll ask, "Do you think he's okay?" since I'm a worrier and his well-being is constantly on my mind. Peter always answers that yes, he's okay, he's safe, he's happy. Peter reminds me that, in fact, Jasper lives better than 99 percent of all living organisms have throughout history.

One of us will say, "What about that time when…" and then we can take that trip down memory lane about when he learned to jump in the pool, tried to get in the gardener's golf cart at Central Park, or got to ride in a taxi down Broadway with his dog walker. It's a nonstop source of entertainment and fun chatter. To us, he's a four-legged Netflix.

When Peter and I talk on the phone during the day, he knows I'm not really calling to see how he's doing, though I go through the motions and ask. I really want to know how Jasper is.

But I mask my question, making it sound like I'm asking after the well-being of my husband. Still, when I ask, "Is everything okay?" Peter knows I'm not asking about the leaking faucet or if the bills have been paid.

"Yes, Jasper is fine. He had a big walk and a chew and is now sitting on the little chair having a snooze." And then, satisfied that all is well at home, I can get back to work.

Everything is okay. That's one of my favorite phrases in the English language. (The other one is "Gutfeld called in sick today.")

"The Vizsla"

(TO THE TUNE OF "THE BOXER"
BY SIMON AND GARFUNKEL)

I am just a Vizsla, and my story's often told
'Cause I'm on my mommy's Twitter
And I'm really rather famous at just four years
old.

Simon and Garfunkel? Or Dana and Jasper?

    * * *

It's really fun

* * *

She puts me on her One More Thing and shows how fast I run.

* * *

Do dee do do do do do dee do…

* * *

When I joined this lovely family, I was no more than a pup
I was all blue eyes and wrinkles
And they fell for me completely when they picked me up.

* * *

I had no fear

* * *

And they never even mentioned that I have a little ear…

* * *

Do dee do do do do do dee do…

* * *

Now I love South Carolina, and I still love Central Park
I go walking with my daddy
They are both big open spaces where I run and bark

* * *

I love to play

* * *

But there's times when I'm so lazy I just lie around all day
And I never snore, no matter what they say...

* * *

I'm America's Dog Jasper, and people think I'm cool,
When they see me in the sidecar, or jumping fifteen feet into the swimming pool
Or on TV with mommy, I live my life in style
But I'm just a happy puppy making everybody smile.

Speak softly
and carry
a big stick.

Jasper and Water

I love to watch dogs playing in water.

Henry could swim with such strength and had such stamina that when we lived in San Diego, he would often surprise the surfers who were out there beyond the break, looking for the next big one. Henry could

catch those waves and ride them in, bodysurfing all the way to the shore. He could also put his head under water, looking for rocks. He'd hold his breath for up to twenty seconds, and sometimes he'd come back up with the rock we'd just thrown in for him. We took him swimming as often as we could.

Henry was an excellent swimmer.

Since Henry loved the water and was a natural swimmer, we thought Jasper would be as well. Not so much.

His first experience with water was at three months old at Ari Fleischer's annual Fourth of July party in Pound Ridge, New York. Ari, another former White House press secretary, said we could bring Jasper, so we took a drive up to visit. I was keeping a watchful eye on my dog so that he didn't steal anyone's food or get underfoot amongst the guests.

The Fleischers had a new swimming pool, and a few people were having some summer fun.

I tried to let Jasper explore without saying no all the time, so he was in front of me trotting along when all of a sudden he was close to the edge of the pool but kept walking. He didn't recognize water and so he just plopped right in. I gasped but didn't want to make a scene. So I reached in and pulled him out by his collar. I held him away from me and kissed his face, not wanting to get wet but wanting him to know that it was okay. He looked stunned.

We went to find Peter.

"What happened?" he asked.

"Tell you later. I need a drink," I said.

Later that night, Peter got Jasper into the pool and helped him try to learn to swim. The dog paddle is never pretty, but with a three-month-old puppy, it sure is cute.

Jasper played in the water later that summer in Annapolis, but it was October before he had his next chance to swim. It didn't go that well, either.

We went to visit Ingrid Henrichsen, a new friend whom I'd met in the city, and her husband, Ward Marsh. They invited us up for a day to a country area near Kent, Connecticut, where Jasper could run around and have a swim in the big pond.

I was excited to have some time with Ingrid and Ward. She and I became close quickly. We call each other sister-friends.

We arrived in this beautiful spot with lots of the autumn leaves still on

Jasper and I before Jasper's disastrous first swim. Well, disastrous for Peter, who had to jump in the lake to rescue him!

the trees. It was the day before Hurricane Sandy, and the weather was still, as if taking a deep breath before the historic storm.

The first thing we did was walk down to the water's edge, making small talk.

Jasper scampered around, and Peter picked up a stick and threw it near the water's edge a few times. Jasper would bring it back, playing a proper game of fetch.

Gradually, Peter tossed the stick a little farther into the water. It was shallow, so Jasper was only getting his legs wet.

And then Peter threw it just a bit too far.

We all had our eyes on Jasper as we talked, and we saw how quickly the water became deep, because all of a sudden, Jasper was splashing and trying to reach the ground.

We called him back to the shore, offering encouragement. He splashed more. And harder. His little legs were working like crazy to keep him up.

I was getting nervous but wasn't panicking…yet.

Jasper instinctively knew what to do and tried to dog paddle, but he was completely vertical, so instead of moving forward, he was just slowly going down. Farther and farther.

"Peter," I said, in that mom voice that alerts a dad.

Peter didn't make a move.

"Peter," I said more firmly and urgently.

I saw Peter had already taken the car keys, phone, and money clip from his pocket and removed his shoes. But to the nervous mother he was in slow motion, and I thought my puppy was going to drown.

"PETER!" I screamed, and just then Peter plunged into the pond and grabbed Jasper, setting him at the correct angle so that his natural swimming instinct took him back to safe ground.

Jasper wasn't fazed. He just ran around with his stick, apparently very proud of himself.

Meanwhile, Peter was coming out of the water, gasping for breath. He was freezing and soaking wet.

Ingrid went into action, demanding that Peter get up to the cabin and take his clothes off.

"But Ingrid, we've just met," he said, keeping his sense of humor.

We got Peter dry and thankfully Ward had an extra set of clothes. Unfortunately for Peter, Ward is much taller and bigger than he is, and so we had to roll up his pants and use Peter's belt to cinch in the waist. The polo shirt was so big it nearly came to Peter's knees. He looked hilarious, and we tried not to laugh but even Peter got the joke.

Peter in Ward's clothes after jumping in the lake to save Jasper. Can you tell Ward is taller than Peter?

And that was the beginning of a beautiful friendship with Ingrid and Ward. And our visits often involve Jasper and swimming in some way.

The next summer, Jasper was reluctant to get into a friend's pool in South Carolina. The young teen boy that lived there, Thomas Gulbin, tried to coax him in, but Jasper was too nervous. It was pitiful, and I was sad because I'd hoped he'd love the water as much as Henry had.

Thomas was undeterred. He asked us if he could take care of Jasper the next afternoon, and we said sure since we were on vacation and wanted to go to Daufuskie Island.

Later that day, we went back to pick Jasper up and we were shocked. There, with Thomas, was Jasper leaping several feet into the air and plunging into the pool. In under an hour, Thomas had taught Jasper to love to swim, and now it's his favorite thing to do. I love to post pictures and videos of his dives, and friends of mine thank me because their young children love to watch the "woof woof videos" on their phones.

Despite his early misgivings, Jasper is now a true water dog.

CLOCKWISE FROM TOP LEFT: *Oh the joy of summer! Jasper and our friend Macy jumping into the water in South Carolina.*
A close-up of Jasper jumping into the pool—look at that focus!
Peter is my "Jasper Jump" photographer. He took this shot from inside the pool.

Not Just a City Dog

Jasper isn't just a city dog. He loves the countryside, too. That's especially true for the Lowcountry of South Carolina, where we like to spend a lot of time. Peter will drive Jasper down for a two- or three-week period and I'll join them on the weekends (great deal if you can get it, Peter!).

Jasper has the instincts of a pointer, and in the city he points at pigeons, squirrels, and even the occasional passing helicopter. In the country, he applies the same skills to fox squirrels, herons, and deer.

On his first official hunt, he was pretty good at flushing out the birds, but he ran back to me upon hearing the first gunshot (I guess that part of him is not so southern). It made me feel loved that he was still his mama's boy.

In South Carolina, Jasper is the reason we met several of our friends. At a crab cake social (it's the South!) we went to one Fourth of July, Jasper pulled toward a Brittany Spaniel named Grady. They became best friends—we call them Grasper. And we became close with his parents, Tracy and Jeff Schyberg, and their daughter, Macy, is like a niece to us now. They introduced us to the Meighans, who have a Vizsla named Bella, and the Gulbins, who have Cassie (and the pool where Jasper learned to swim, jump, and dive). From there we met even more people, and we enjoy the area so much that we count the days until we're able to be back to see them all.

Jasper thrives in the Lowcountry. He runs like the wind amongst the live oaks covered in Spanish moss and through the pine tree stands. We let him look for fish in the saltwater, but keep him away from the ponds with

Team Grasper is ready to go kayaking!

alligators; we've put the fear of God into him whenever he gets near that water.

Once we took him kayaking on the May River during low tide, and we let Jasper run like mad on the sandbar. He was in his element, chasing the jumping fish. I'd never seen his natural instincts take over like that. He was powerful. And fast. But he was running over the oyster beds and we knew that could be dangerous for dogs.

As we headed back to the dock, Peter called to me. "Dana, there's blood everywhere. And it isn't mine."

We paddled as fast as we could back to shore. Then we got him out of the kayak. I also knew he had to pee, but I couldn't carry him, so I just rushed as quickly as we could up to the grass. He left bloody paw prints all the way up the dock.

After Peter and Dr. Jeff, Grady's dad and a physician, came off the dock, we turned Jasper over and the cuts were deep in two paws.

Jasper didn't make a sound, but it looked very painful. Jeff treated him and came by regularly to change the bandages and check on the wounds. Jasper was down for the count for about a week and received strong antibiotics from the vet. He spent hours quietly sitting, looking a little pitiful, and getting sympathetic messages from all around the world.

Thankfully, he healed quickly and there was no permanent damage. We city folk learned our lesson that day—dogs should never get to run on sandbars where there are oyster shell beds.

In South Carolina, he spends his afternoons out on the porch, watching the world go by (a Carolina specialty). If we make a move toward the back door, he darts out before we do so that he

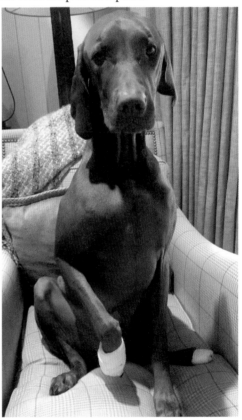

Bandaged paws after getting cut on the oyster shells in South Carolina. Sadly, no pearls were found . . . except this guy.

won't be left behind. On some of our bike rides, we go slowly so that he and Grady can trot alongside us up the road.

But Jasper's very favorite thing to do, and for which he's become quite famous, is to ride in the sidecar of Peter's Harley.

Peter had long wanted to replace the motorcycle he sold when I lived in England with him and needed a car. I'd said I didn't mind if he got one, but what was he going to do, leave Jasper behind on his rides? He'd already thought of a solution. He planned to buy a retired police cruiser with a sidecar. As luck would have it, there was one for sale in Savannah, Georgia. (When a man really wants something, he can find it!)

When he brought the bike home, Jasper was afraid of the noise at first. But he wanted to be with his dad. So I got into the sidecar and Peter lifted Jasper in and he sat between my legs. From then on, the Harley has been Jasper's domain. He lives to go for a ride.

Peter bought him some Doggles and Jasper didn't even flinch when we put them on, as if he knew he couldn't ride without them. He looked like Snoopy fighting the Red Baron. I even tied a scarf around his neck.

Look out Sons of Anarchy . . .

The first summer Peter had the bike, Jasper and he rode in the local Fourth of July parade. Sadly, my flight had been canceled due to weather and I was stuck in New York, so I didn't see it. I hated to miss it—especially because Jasper won Best Dog at the parade. We proudly

Jasper and Peter on the Fourth of July in the superhero parade.

display his trophy on the mantel. And every time we're there for a visit and take him for a ride, folks point and laugh and clap. I can't tell if Jasper is performing—but I know Peter is (and I love him for it).

When Jasper's not out riding or running around and I'm there, he will sit on the porch bed swing with me. He's good company when I'm writing and working. I wrote most of *And the Good News Is . . .* with him by my side on the second floor, watching all the folks riding by on their bikes and walking their dogs. We'd just sway side to side since the swing can't go forward and back because of a wall. He's as content to sit with me as he is eager to get outside.

In the evenings, we take the dogs down to the fire pits by the river and we let them wander around while people enjoy making s'mores and having a nightcap. There's a mix of locals and tourists, lots of kids and dogs. We enjoy it when people recognize Jasper and ask to get a picture taken with him (he charges them in graham crackers). Jasper, of course, is eager to find as many broken cracker bits as he can. We turn a blind eye if someone gives him an extra one.

In South Carolina, we've found the perfect place to live the life we want—one that fully incorporates our dog. We're surrounded by neighbors and friends who feel the same way about their pets, so everyone gets along and helps watch out for the dogs. In fact, hardly anyone ever leaves a dog alone there. We can always drop Jasper off with a neighbor if we have to run into town, or we leave at least two dogs together so that they have company (which may explain the new generation of mixed breeds running around).

No one thinks we're strange or over the top with our dog there. Well… not that we've heard. They may just be too polite to say anything.

When Peter and Jasper drive home, they usually do it over two days to break up the long road trip. Jasper can get restless in the car, so Peter stops often and lets him wander around and stretch his four legs. Then last winter, when I called to check on their progress, Peter said that Jasper was panting a lot and that he was a bit worried. Of course that meant I was sick to my stomach wondering what could be wrong. Thankfully, it wasn't an illness; instead, Peter realized that he'd accidentally turned on the rear heated seats in our new vehicle. Jasper was melting from the inside out and had no way to alert the driver. The good news was he got to ride with his head out of the window for the rest of the way home.

A superior traveling companion we couldn't ask for. Whether we're in the city or the country, Jasper makes everywhere a better place.

A city dog by day; a country dog at heart.

A Day in the Life of Jasper

(AS TOLD BY

JASPER PERINO)

5 a.m.—New York City—the city that never sleeps, even if you're dog tired. The trucks start coming by before dawn and when I hear "beep beep beep" I get up from my bed on the floor, stretch upward and downward as dogs do, and walk to my mom's

Jasper sleeping with his sock monkey.

side of the bed—because she never rejects me. I flap my ears, shaking the sleep out of my head. Then I sit and wait for her to say, "Come on up, Jasper." She pats the bed. I don't want to seem too eager, so I wait a couple of beats. "Come ON, Jasper." She can't get back to sleep while I'm just sitting there staring at her, so I hop up.

My mom and I have a routine in the mornings. When I get on the bed, she turns on her side as I twist around finding my spot. "Cuddle in," she says and then I land with a thump, my shoulder blade digging into her stomach, which is the best way to assure I get close enough to her. "Jeez, Jasper," she says. Then she pats my head and puts her arm over my side. She grabs ahold of one of my legs, and my dad lays his hand on top of hers. We sleep for another hour or so, ignoring the horns honking down below as people get their day started.

6:30 a.m.—My dad gets up and opens the window shade so that my mom can watch the sunrise. Then he goes to make her Strawberry Carnation Instant Breakfast and English breakfast tea—he brings it to her in bed, just like his dad did for his mom. They train them well in jolly old England. I open one eye but otherwise don't stir. My mom says her prayers and starts reading the news clips of the day. If I roll over onto my back, she snaps a picture, laughs, and sends it to her girlfriend. She thinks it's their little secret, but I'm on to them. Eat your hearts out, ladies.

7:30 a.m.—Dog park! Central Park is leash-free from 6 to 9 a.m. every day. Morning walks are my favorites. Usually my dad takes me while my mom pitches stories for *The Five* and posts pictures he sends to her. We walk about three miles. We stop at the pond to look at the fish, then we walk up to Bethesda Fountain near Big Dog Hill and back to the baseball fields. That's where I run around with my pack, an assortment of terriers, poodles, ridgebacks, whippets, and shepherds. I've known most of these dogs all my life. There's Hershey, Lily, Zeke, EZ, Otto, Bear, Bella, Martina—and many more. Our play fighting looks and sounds vicious, especially in slo-mo video, but we'd never hurt a fly. When we get home, my dad makes my breakfast and my mom wants a full report. It's funny to hear him tell her what happened—as if he knows what we were thinking! On weekends when she joins us at the park, I show off a bit with leaps over tall fences and what they call my "Silly Two Minutes" on the ivy near the bridge.

9 a.m.–1 p.m.—A dog's gotta nap. After breakfast I usually hang on the couch with my dad while he works on his laptop. He doesn't mind too much when I want a little attention and lay my head down on his keyboard. I've been on more than a few Skype calls with his clients. Sometimes he plays a YouTube video for me because I like to watch puppies playing—it never gets old.

1 p.m.–2 p.m. I can't read a clock but I can tell time. Around 1:00, I start listening for the elevator because that's when my dog walker, Barbara Stevenson, comes to pick me up. I love Barbara! I always greet her with a toy, such as my sock monkey or moose.

Barbara and I cover a lot of ground, from Central Park West to Broadway to Columbus Circle and then back through the park where I stalk a few squirrels and pigeons. I like to keep my hunting skills sharp in case I ever need to use them. Occasionally, she hails a taxi and rolls down the window for me to stick my head out for the ride to pick up another dog. I pretend not to see the tourists who point and laugh—have they never seen a dog in a cab?

2 p.m.–5 p.m.—More napping, this time on the bed or the chair. I especially like to lie on the clean laundry—it smells so good. Sometimes I stand on the ottoman that was supposed to be for my mom's feet to rest, but she gave it to me so that I can look out the window and see what's going on out there. Often I'll go with my dad to run an errand. My favorite is the bank where the folks there have treats for me. I'm supposed to get only one, but with this face I always get two. We also go to the post office, and I sit at my dad's feet while he mails packages. I try to blend into the carpet because I'm not supposed to be inside. Once when he was told there were no dogs allowed, my dad in his British accent said I was a therapy dog. Which is true, in a way, since I tend to make people feel better.

Just another day at the bank.

5 p.m.—Every day my dad has this ritual to sit on the sofa and watch *The Five*. He types notes about the show and sends them to my mom during the commercial breaks. A few times, I've had the chance to go to her studio and sit in for a segment of the show. That's always fun. I'm a bit of a natural, actually—I just sit there and look into the camera and people kind of love it. My mom makes me wear a tie when I'm on set—she's a bit old-fashioned that way.

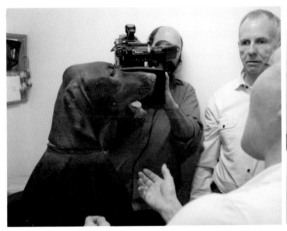

ABOVE LEFT: *Jasper getting his hair and makeup done before going on set.*
ABOVE RIGHT: *Jasper in the Green Room before his appearance on* The Five.
BELOW LEFT: *Jasper on* The Five, *in his bow tie, of course!*
BELOW RIGHT: *Jasper comes on set of* The Five *for his birthday.*

6 p.m.—My internal clock tells me it's time to head out with my dad to meet my mom at Columbus Circle as she walks home. I never quite know when she's going to appear, so I'm on full alert. And when I see her—oh it's crazy. My tail wags me all around. I jump up and grab onto her hips, trying not to knock out one of her teeth when I reach up for a kiss (she's my mom!)—I'm just so enthusiastic sometimes I can't help it. She never gets mad at me, though. It makes me think that I should try to get away with more.

7-10 p.m. I like it when my parents stay home in the evenings. My mom takes off her TV makeup and changes into something comfy. Then she sits on her side of the couch and I scramble up to nuzzle in as we watch the last part of *Special Report*. She's always telling my dad to shush when this guy Charles Krauthammer starts talking. I guess he's a genius, at least that's what she says. After Charles is finished, I get to have my dinner. Meat and kibble—it always tastes so good!

My favorite show is *Wheel of Fortune*, which they watch after *Jeopardy!* (That show is too hard for me.) I get a kick out of Pat Sajak—it's like he's always just about to tell a joke. That guy's got the life—what a job!

Before we settle in to watch some shows, one of my parents gets on the floor by my toy box and we have a big game of tug-of-war. I can pull my mom across the floor, which she thinks is hilarious. My dad's trick is to hide a toy under his torso, and I humor him for a bit until I really want it back. Then I lick his ears, which makes him crack up and he drops his guard. I win every time.

I watch TV for a while and my parents do some last-minute work. Then my mom asks my dad to "help us" and he gets up and moves me around until I'm on my back and she can hold me like she did when I was a pup. It's pretty sweet. We stay like that until it's time for my "last wee." Sometimes I just can't be bothered because I'm so cozy, so my dad has to play a game of hide-and-seek with me. I've always been scared that they're going to leave me, so he knows I'll jump up to make sure he hasn't disappeared into thin air.

We head down in the elevator where I sit and look at my dad's pocket. I wait for him to say his line, "What do we do in the elevator?" Well, I sit and then he produces a biscuit, broken in half, so it feels like I'm getting two treats. It's a play that's run off-Broadway every day of my life.

Once my dad forgot something in the apartment and he left me in the hallway after he called for the elevator. He wasn't back by the time the doors opened, and on instinct I stepped inside. Then the doors shut behind me. I'd never been in an elevator on my own before. I tried to be brave but I started to panic as the elevator went down. I looked at the buttons, but it was all Greek to me. Suddenly the car stopped and then started going back up. The doors opened on our floor and my dad was there saying, "Oh thank God, Jasper! Are you okay?" But he was laughing, too. When we got upstairs that night, he told my mom what happened. Let's just say that she didn't think it was funny. She really let him have it!

Aside from mishaps like that night, our last trip outside goes smoothly. I hurry to get my business done so that we can go back upstairs to my mom. She always gives me a bit of her hand lotion before we go to sleep—I lick it off my paws so that I won't try to lick her hands. Pretty smart on her part—it's what they call a win-win. Kind of like my life with them. 🐾

Jasper's face when I met the late Jake-Dierks Bentley's dog, in Nashville.

Jasper Grows Up

'**ve always been interested in time—how it passes, how we remember it,
when it slows and when it flies. In fact, time was the subject of my speech
that won the Colorado state speech and debate tournament in 1990. And
so while I know there's nothing I can do to slow down the clock on life, I
can't help but look at Jasper and worry about the end of his.

Paw prints in the sand. One of my favorite photos from the beach in Quogue, NY.

Jasper is four years old now. No longer a puppy but young enough to have a puppy's characteristics. Jasper's lean, athletic, and strong. "Fit as a butcher's dog," Peter says. And except for the occasional cut paw or stomach bug (called collywobbles in England), he's healthy.

He hardly ever needs a telling off—he's well behaved and easy to take care of. We take him with us into shops that allow dogs, and he's an angel. Everyone loves him. (Especially the ladies. I tell my single male friends that they should take him out to the park for a couple of hours—they are destined to meet a few young ladies on that walk.)

I can tell he's older now, because he sleeps a bit longer and doesn't need to go out as much as he did as a youngster. And he can be left on his own for a couple of hours without any problems (except for the occasional protest pee in South Carolina when he knows he's missing out).

And I also know he's aging because I can see little white bits of

Strike a pose: Jasper playing in his bed. Notice that, in deference to Gutfeld, I cropped the junk out.)

Coppertone Dog.

fur growing under his chin and in tiny spots on his cheeks and his paws. It crushes me. I don't want him to grow old. I want him to always be my puppy Jasper. And I get a lump in my throat when I think about it. Dog owners always count the years.

My head tells me I just need to enjoy him fully and to take good care of him and not worry about the end, but my heart…well, it breaks because of the inevitable.

That's one of the reasons I'm so excited to share these stories with you. Writing about Joco, Henry, and Jasper commemorates them on the page. And it makes me realize how blessed and full of love my life is.

So enjoy Jasper, America. He is our dog.

Introducing
@FiveFanPhotoshops

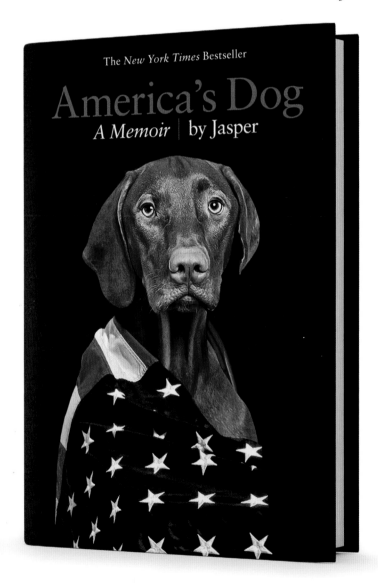

When Jasper was about five months old, I started seeing posts on Twitter from someone named "FiveFanPhotoshops." The tweets took photos of Jasper, a co-host of *The Five,* or someone from the cast of *Red Eye*, and Photoshopped them into other scenes, often relevant to something we'd just talked about on the show or a major event, like a holiday, movie release, or sporting competition. The work was excellent and laugh-out-loud funny. And I had no idea who was posting them. Every time I saw one, it was like getting a surprise gift.

I retweeted the photos, and my followers loved them. Jasper's fan base grew. And I was a direct beneficiary when it came to growing my number of Twitter followers.

When I added a Facebook page, I noticed that any post about Jasper would get tons of likes and comments, but anything I posted about politics or even mentoring advice for young professionals didn't get as much attention. However, if I posted something that FiveFan had created, it almost broke the Internet á la Kim Kardashian.

Over time, I realized that Jasper and FiveFan had done something for me that I hadn't been able to do for myself—given me an avenue where there was less work and more joy, more laughs, and an additional identity beyond politics. I realized I had a whole new direction in which to grow and have fun.

I figured out how to connect with FiveFan, and we were fast friends. Now I count him among one of my few confidants.

FiveFan stays anonymous because he wants to. He is clever. He's a talented artist. Beyond creative. And self-taught in Photoshop. I've never known anyone so exceedingly humble. He's also very generous. He'll willingly make a custom Photoshop for me if I get a wild idea. For example, one year I had an idea of giving out nice bottles of wine for Christmas, and I asked if he could make a label of Jasper as James Bond. About thirty-five minutes later, he sent a finished product.

"Something like this?" he asked.

Peter and I were amazed. "How does he do that?"

I asked him how it all started, and he said it was in 2012, on the final night of the Republican National Convention. A big "mystery speaker" was set to talk, and on *The Five,* we kicked it around the table, wondering who it should be.

"When it came to Dana, she said the Republican who would really bring down the house was . . . Jasper! Greg groaned, and he asked how she knew he was a Republican. "I told him so."

That's when FiveFan said the image of Jasper speaking onstage at the RNC immediately started forming in his mind, so he opened Photoshop and started putting it together. He placed Jasper behind the lectern, changed the signs in the crowd to read "Jasper!" switched out the Teleprompters for tennis balls, and added Greg protesting that *he* should have been the speaker.

"It was a lot of fun to make," he said.

The quality of FiveFan's work is impressive, even to experts of the software program. I asked him how he became so proficient.

"I had been using Photoshop for about ten years, doing graphic design and making websites. I never had any formal training, just learned how to use it over time," he said. He added that there's always something more to learn and to improve. Isn't that true for all of us?

So how did he become FiveFanPhotoshop?

"You can tell I didn't put too much thought into my Twitter name: 'Hmm, I'm a fan of this show called *The Five*, and I'll probably be doing some Photoshops...'" So he's logical, too. "From there I kept up doing Photoshops revolving around things said on *The Five*, or my other favorite show, *Red Eye*, with plenty of Jasper adventures thrown in the mix. It was fun to interact with the shows that way, and I was amazed when Dana started showing some of my little Photoshops as her One More Thing feature on the show."

When I decided to do this book, I wanted to do something more than just write my story. I wanted to show it. I wanted to make people chuckle and get a real kick out of these pictures. FiveFan agreed to partner with me, and this book is a product of our friendship. I'm honored to know him. Readers and Jasper fans, the real treat of this book follows. Featured here is the talented work of @FiveFanPhotoshops: pictures that will make you smile, even laugh out loud. I hope you enjoy them as much as I do.

Portraits of a Dog

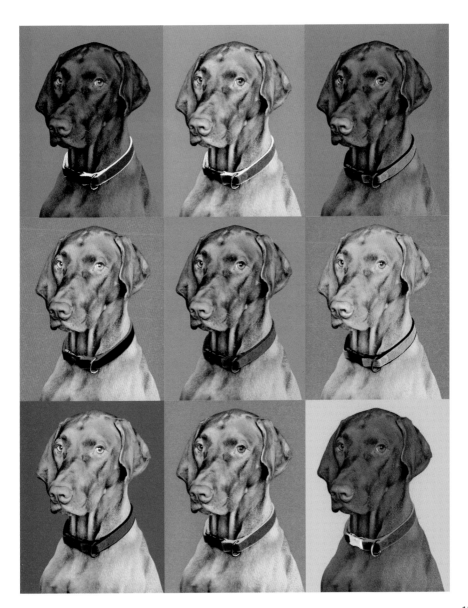

137

Play Like a Champion,
Train Like an Underdog

147

159

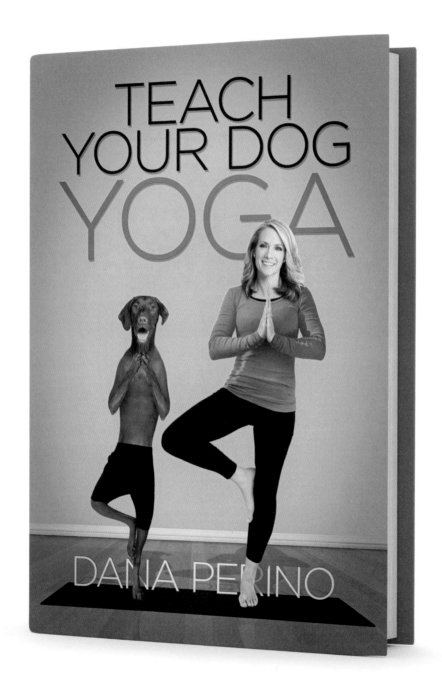

TEACH YOUR DOG YOGA

DANA PERINO

169

Jingle Bells and Jack-o-Lanterns

175

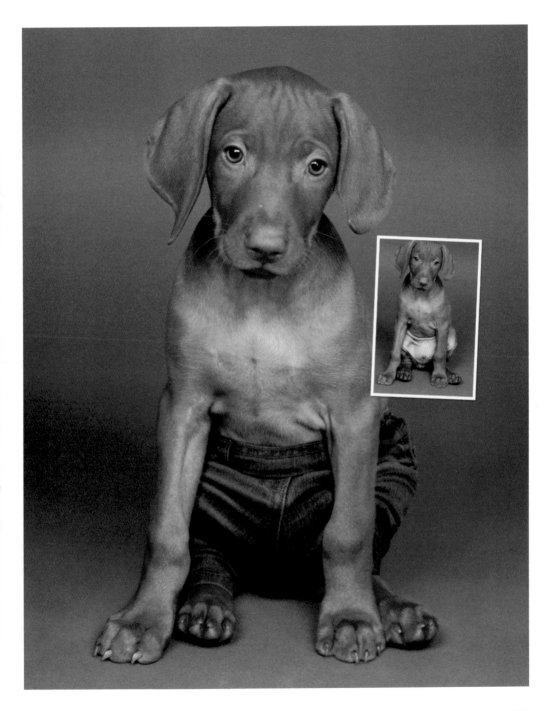

JASPER M.D.

185

Collect Them All!

JASPER
AMERICA'S DOG
Cotton Dress Socks

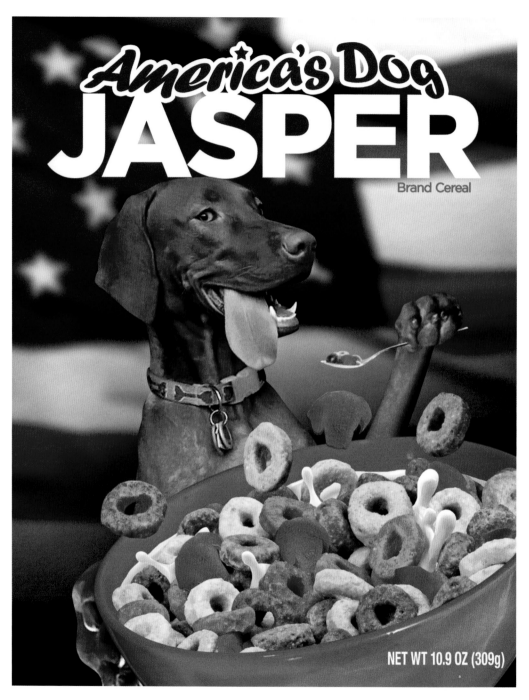

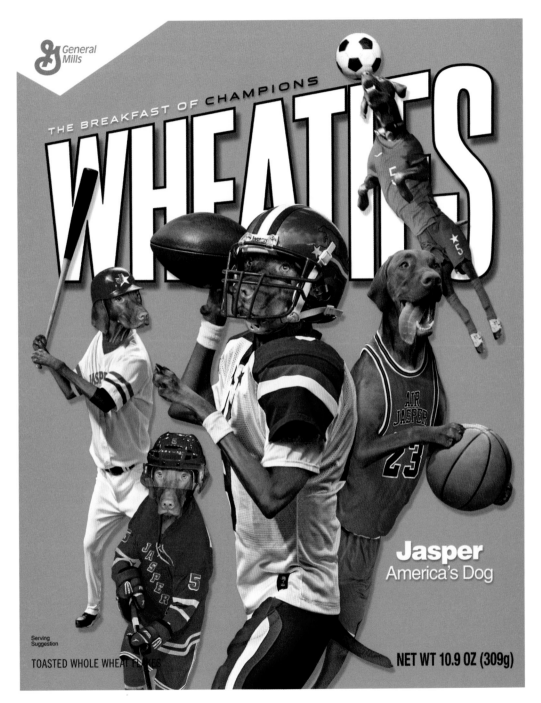

iJasper

Every iJasper is pre-loaded with over 50 gigabytes of Jasper photos

203

Political Hot Dog

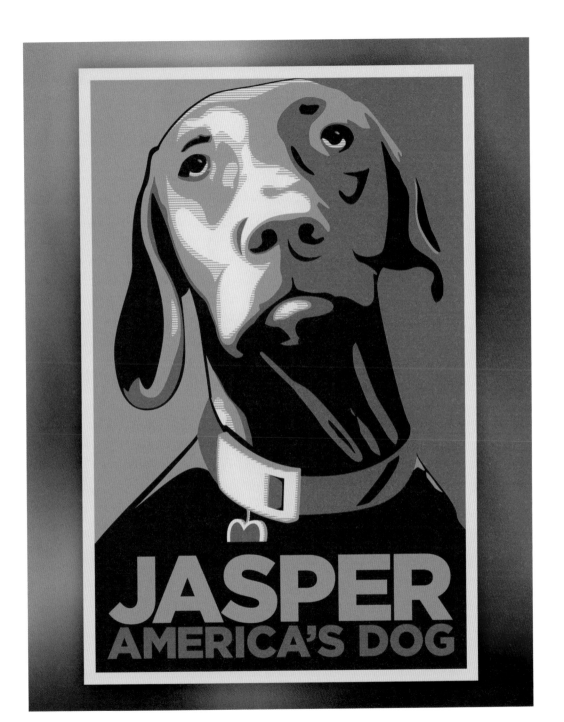

Debate prep.

211

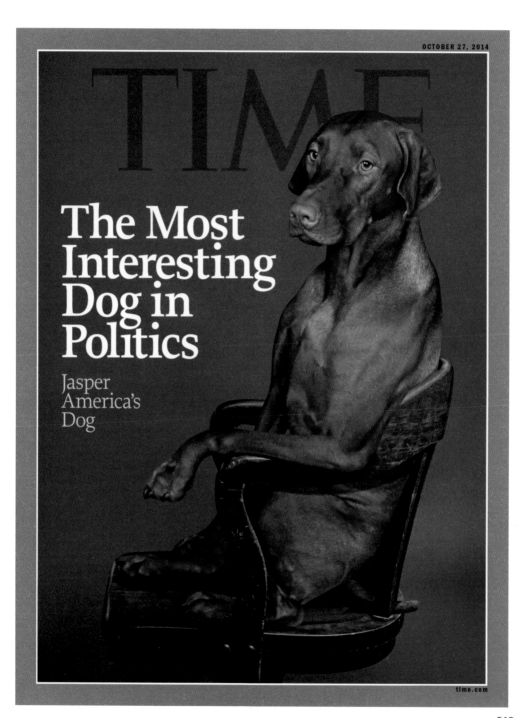

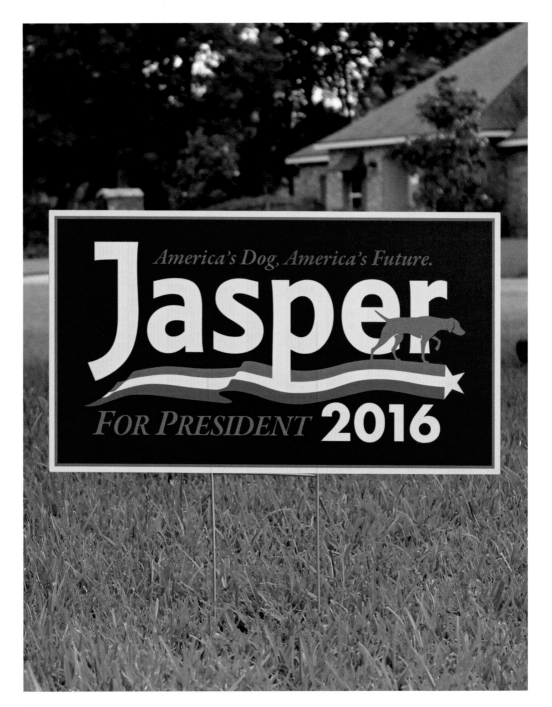

DANA PERINO

Jasper & Me

LIFE AND LOVE WITH THE WORLD'S GREATEST DOG

Dana Perino

FORMER WHITE HOUSE PRESS SECRETARY
AND JASPER'S MOM

And the
Good News Is...

Lessons and Advice from the Bright Side

Special
Collector's
Edition

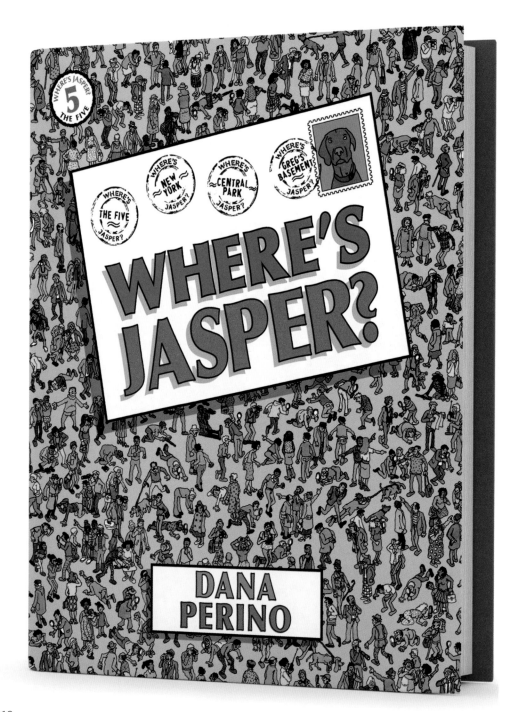

HOSTED BY **DANA PERINO**
— THE —

JASPERS

LIVE JASPER SUNDAY FEB 24 7e|4p

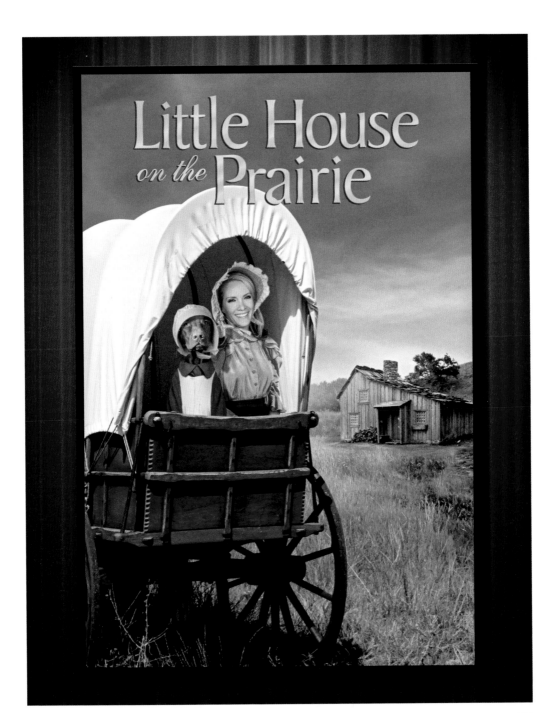

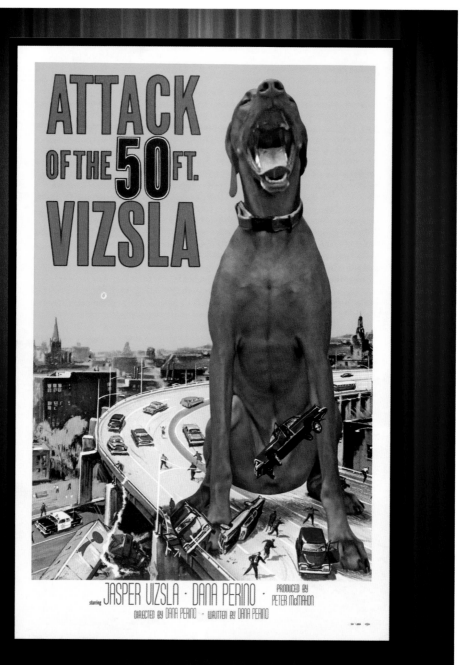

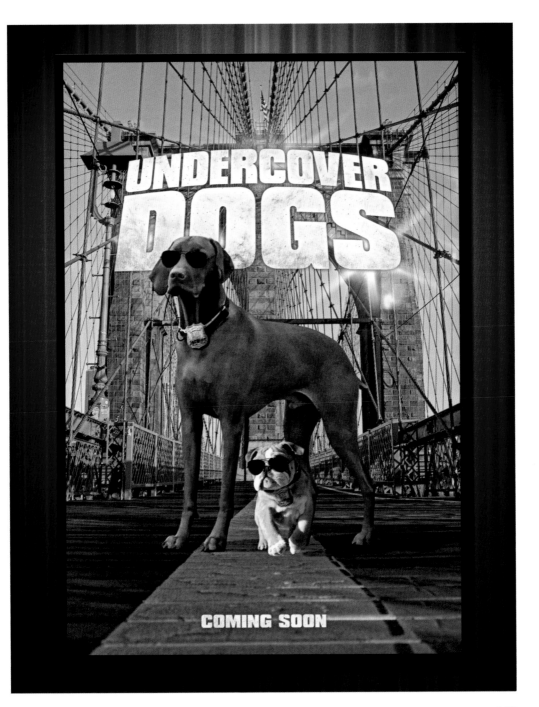

225

"A MOVING 3 YEAR EPIC
THAT ISN'T QUITE LIKE ANYTHING ELSE IN THE HISTORY OF CINEMA"
JASPER VIZSLA
DANA PERINO
PETER McMAHON
PUPPYHOOD
Written and Directed by
Dana Perino
THE FIVE PRESENTS A FOX NEWS PRODUCTION A FILM BY DANA PERINO "PUPPYHOOD" JASPER VIZSLA DANA PERINO PETER McMAHON GREG GUTFELD
MUSIC BY DIERKS BENTLEY DANA PERINO DIRECTOR OF PHOTOGRAPHY PETER McMAHON EXECUTIVE PRODUCERS KIMBERLY GUILFOYLE ERIC BOLLING BRIAN KILMEADE JAUN WILLIAMS
FOX NEWS SCREENPLAY BY DANA PERINO PRODUCED BY DANA PERINO DIRECTED BY DANA PERINO THE FIVE

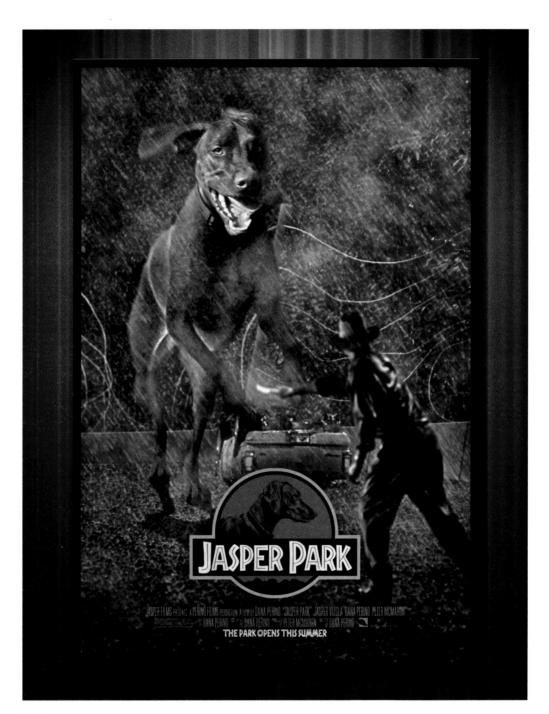

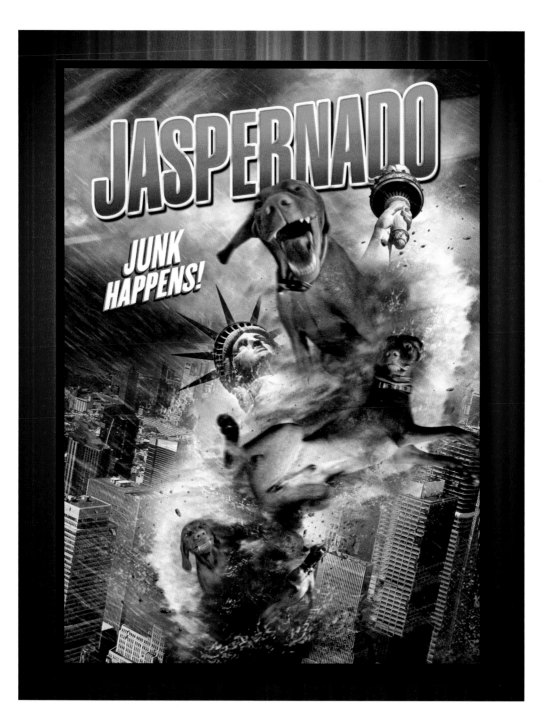

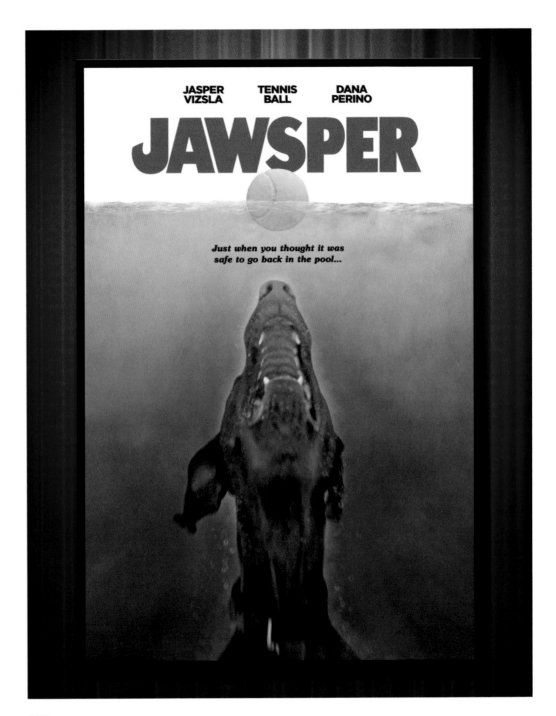

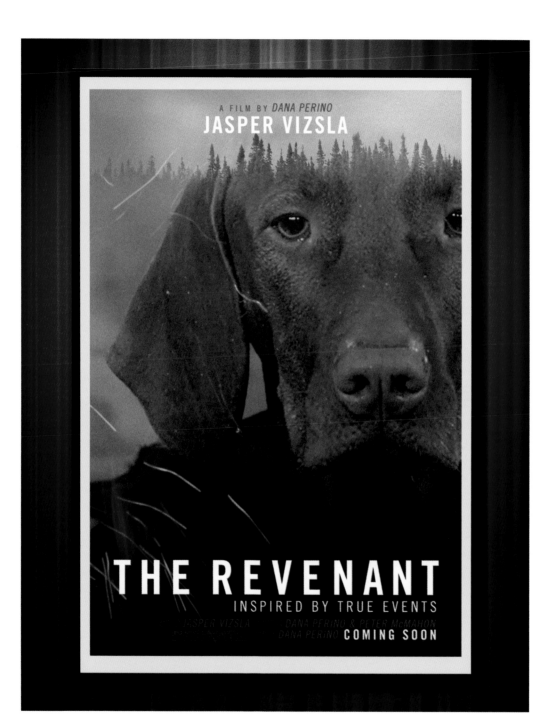

The Dogfather

Jasper Vizsla

Peter McMahon   Dana Perino   Dana Perino ...... Jasper Vizsla   'The Dogfather'   Color by Technicolor   A Dana Perino Picture

PG PARENTAL GUIDANCE SUGGESTED
SOME MATERIAL MAY NOT BE SUITABLE FOR CHILDREN

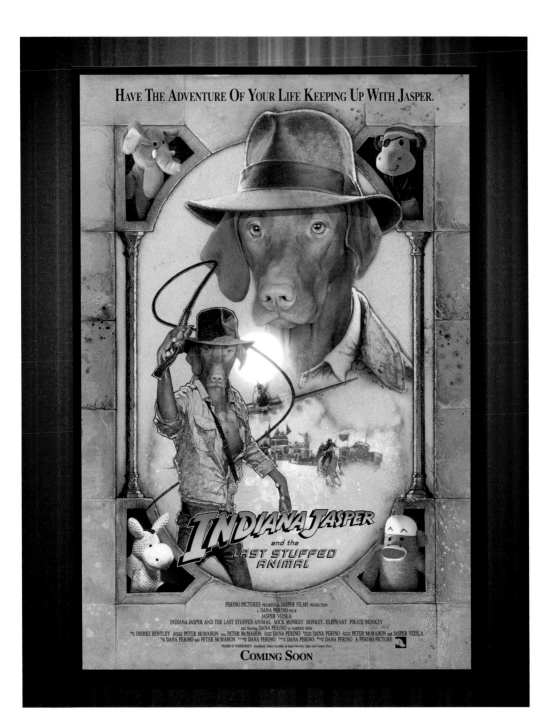

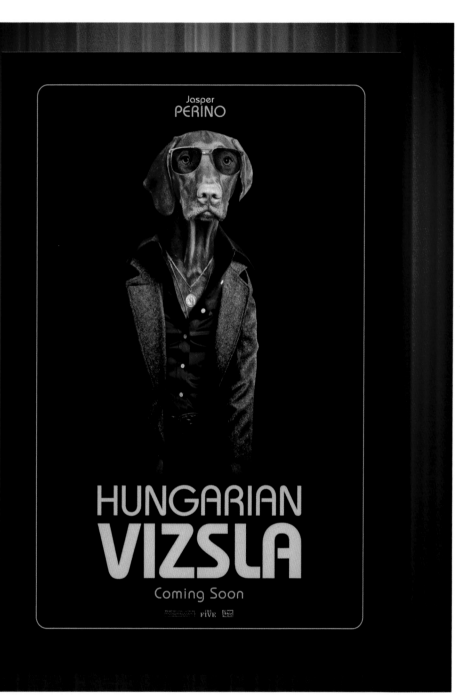

234

235

236

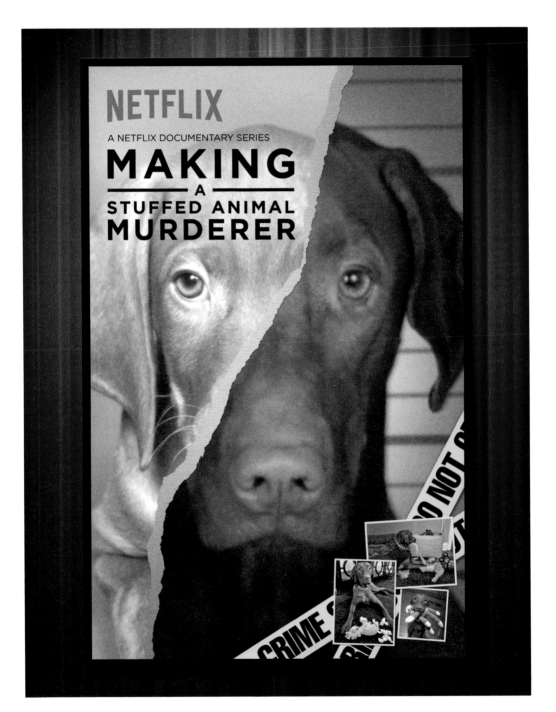

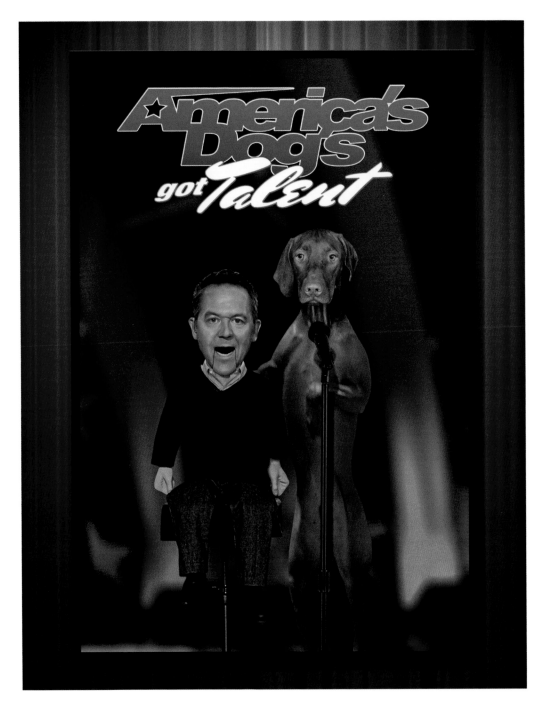

239

COOKING
with Jasper

Jasper's Glamorous TV Life

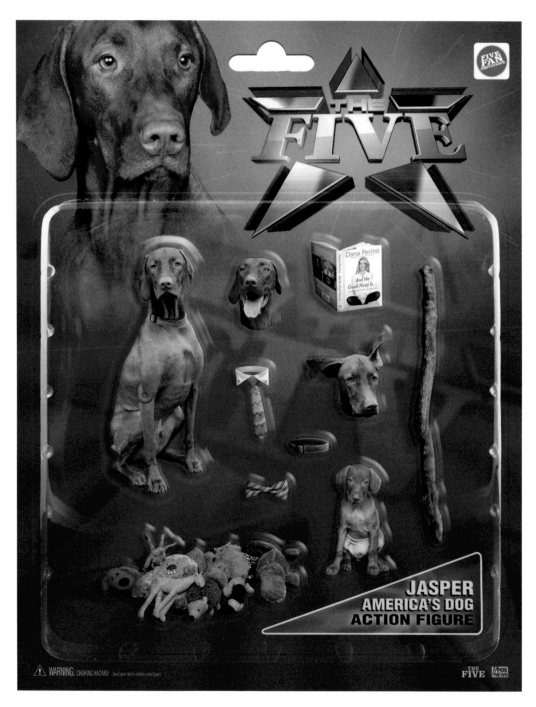

248

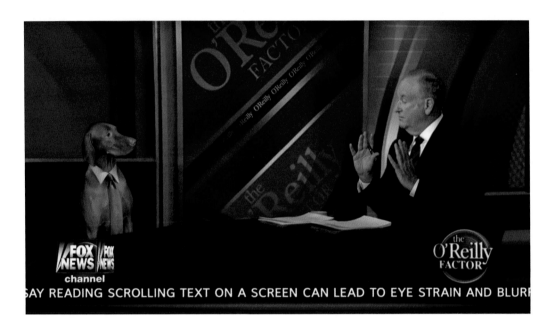

Jasper's Acknowledgments

Grady Martina Bella Zeke Lily

Honey Lilly Tucker Hershey EZ

Bella Bear

Cassie Princess

256

Acknowledgments

My gratitude abounds.

Thanks to Bob Barnett, who cheerfully helps guide my career and is forever on my side.

Erin Landers, of Dana Perino and Company. Peter says she reminds him of me when we first met (when I was nice!). Erin's enthusiasm, judgment, and creative talents have raised the bar. "Oh, it was easy," she says. Thank you, Erin.

At Twelve, thanks to Publisher Deb Futter, a wonderful champion for her authors. I like how we communicate with our eyes—she gets me. Sean Desmond, my editor and very good friend, was true to his word: "There will be a dog book." I'm always glad when he calls (I've never sent him to voicemail). Libby Burton has the perfect editing touch and cheerful disposition. Jarrod Taylor was patient while I decided on which of his great covers to choose. Brian McLendon is such a dog lover that he wanted to do this book first, before *And the Good News Is. . . .* Paul Samuelson puts up with a former White House press secretary who thinks she knows about public relations, and Bailey Donoghue is a steady hand with a bright future.

Paul Mauro helped me lighten the copy. If you laughed, that was likely his edit. His wife, Joan McNaughton, is our courier and never complains about the extra work I send his way.

Melanie Dunea did the cover shot for both of my books. I'm sure you can guess why we keep calling her back.

Friends deserving of special mention are Tim and Michelle Chase and their boys, Ryan, Benjamin, and William. They love Jasper like a brother. Nicolle and Mark Wallace are Vizsla enthusiasts who give us a chance to visit their home, where Jasper runs wild with Lilly and Honey (Lilly was Henry's first love during the White House days). Megyn Kelly and Doug Brunt share their considerable talents and care for their friends in special ways. Ingrid Henrichsen, my "sister-friend," and Ward Marsh have known Jasper since he was a puppy and were there for his disastrous first swim, yet they keep inviting us back! Jeff and Tracy Schyberg and their daughter, Macy English, bring us so much joy. Grady is their Brittany Spaniel, and we met when our dogs pulled toward each other at a crab cake social in South Carolina. Grady and Jasper are a unit we call "Grasper."

My trusted readers included several good friends: Charles Blahous, Keith Hennessey, Tony Fratto, Jeanie Mamo, Trey Bohn, Ken Lisaius, and Scott Stanzel.

My thanks to the people whose services we depend upon and who have became dear to us: Kyra Doumele, Laura Garcia, Barbara Stevenson, and John Hernandez.

The Fox News Channel has indulged my love of dogs from the beginning and helped me find joy in a career after the White House.

The Five was supposed to be a temporary five-week show, but we've been going for over five years. My career transition would not have happened without my co-hosts' encouragement. My heartfelt appreciation and regards for Eric Bolling, Kimberly Guilfoyle, Greg Gutfeld, and Juan Williams. And the unsung heroes of the show, the producers: Porter Berry, Megan Albano, Susan Wertheim, Alexandra Novak, Mina Pertesis, Amanda Hooshangi, Sean O'Rourke, Kyle Goodwin, and Emily Cyr.

The crew—especially Michelle Frazzetta, JoJo Rodriguez, Vashti Williams, Allison DeBlois, and Jack Wright—make us look and sound amazing and protect us from embarrassment when coming back from rowdy commercial breaks. Plus they laugh at my corny jokes.

A special thanks to Gutfeld, who made the right call on the cover. Even though he makes fun of me and says he hates Jasper, I think he really wants a dog.

FiveFan, your talent amazes me. I always laugh out loud when you post a Photoshop. I'm glad we are friends, and you're still the best part about Twitter.

To my family who read drafts, dug through photo albums, and joined me on trips down memory lane: Leo Perino, Jan Perino, Ben and Angie Perino Machock, Preston Perino, and Jill Perino Pischke.

Thanks to everyone at the Central Park dog park. You make me love New York.

If you enjoy the photographs of Jasper on social media, chances are my husband, Peter McMahon, took them. He deserves more credit. My stomach still does flips when I remember that I almost missed that flight. He takes good care of us.

Finally, to Jasper. You can't read this (or can you?), but thank you for making my days over and over again. May we have many more healthy years of your goofy and desperate love.